Twayne's United States Authors Series

EDITOR OF THIS VOLUME

Warren French

Indiana University

Luke Short

TUSAS 368

Luke Short

LUKE SHORT

By ROBERT L. GALE

University of Pittsburgh

TWAYNE PUBLISHERS
A DIVISION OF G. K. HALL & CO., BOSTON

Published in 1981 by Twayne Publishers,
A Division of G. K. Hall & Co.
All Rights Reserved

Printed on permanent/durable acid-free paper and bound
in the United States of America

First Printing

Library of Congress Cataloging in Publication Data

Gale, Robert L.
Luke Short.

(Twayne's United States authors series ; TUSAS 368)
Bibliography: p. 171-78
Includes index.
1.   Short, Luke—Criticism and interpretation.
PS3513.L68158Z67   813'.54   80-25827
ISBN 0-8057-7307-X

For Maureen

"And so to study three years is but short"
Shakespeare, *Love's Labour's Lost* (I, i, 180)

For Maureen

"And so to study three years is but short"
Shakespeare, *Love's Labour's Lost* (I, i, 180)

Contents

About the Author

Robert Lee Gale was born in Des Moines, Iowa, and was educated at Dartmouth College (B.A.) and Columbia University (M.A. and Ph.D.). He served in the U.S. Army Counter-Intelligence Corps in Europe during World War II. He has taught at Columbia, the University of Delaware, the University of Mississippi, and the University of Pittsburgh, where he is now professor of American Literature. He has had Fulbright teaching fellowships to Italy and Finland, and has also lectured in Germany, Canada, Denmark, and Russia. Gale is the author of *The Caught Image: Figurative Language in the Fiction of Henry James; Thomas Crawford, American Sculptor; Plots and Characters in Henry James, Plots and Characters in Nathaniel Hawthorne, Plots and Characters in Herman Melville, Plots and Characters in Edgar Allan Poe*, and *Plots and Characters in Mark Twain;* the "Henry James" chapter in *Eight American Authors* (revised edition); Western Writers Series booklets *Charles Warren Stoddard* and *Charles Marion Russell;* and many study guides, critical essays, and reviews. He is currently editing the Archon *Plots and Characters Series*, which will soon number about fifteen volumes. In addition, Gale is the author of the TUSAS volumes on *Richard Henry Dana, Jr., Francis Parkman*, and *John Hay*. He teaches courses and seminars in American literature, especially nineteenth-century fiction, Civil War literature, Western literature, and the Roaring Twenties.

Preface

Frederick Dilley Glidden, better known to millions of readers as Luke Short, was and still is one of the most popular and respected writers of Western fiction America has ever produced. Louis L'Amour, Zane Grey, Max Brand, Luke Short, and Jack Schaefer—probably in about that order—are the best sellers in the field, and together account for sales in excess of 200 million copies, give or take a few tons. These writers sell because they entertain and because they give their readers a thrilling picture of an era which has gone—the late-nineteenth-century American Old West, when the land was glorious, and when men were men, villains were obviously repulsive, action was explosive, and women were beautiful and compliant.

Short published fifty-one novels and about twice that number of short stories. Much of his fiction first appeared, sometimes serially, in the *Saturday Evening Post, Collier's,* and such quality pulp magazines as *Argosy, Blue Book, Star Western,* and *Western Story.* Short's hardbound publishers were Farrar and Rinehart, Doubleday Doran, Macmillan, Houghton Mifflin, Random House, and (in London) Collins and Hammond Hammond. He has been translated into German, French, Norwegian, Spanish, Dutch, and Urdu. He has even been pirated and plagiarized—perhaps the ultimate compliment.

Buffs remember with special fondness such novels of Short's as *Hard Money, Gunman's Chance, Hardcase, Ride the Man Down, Sunset Graze, Ramrod, Coroner Creek, Station West, Ambush,* and *The Whip.* A dozen or so of his novels and stories were made into movies, mostly in the late 1940s and early 1950s. The best were *Ramrod* (starring Joel McCrea), *Blood on the Moon* (based on *Gunman's Chance* and starring Robert Mitchum), *Coroner Creek* (with Randolph Scott), *Station West* (Dick Powell), *Vengeance Valley* (Burt Lancaster), *Ride the Man Down* (George Montgomery), and "The Hangman" (Robert Taylor). In the heyday of TV Westerns in the 1950s, a few of Short's short stories appeared on the "Zane Grey Theater." Short's novels are readily available in inexpensive Bantam, Dell, and Fawcett paperback reprints. *Books in Print* year after year lists fifteen or twenty of his titles, which regularly sell out and are reprinted yet again.

Fred Glidden was born in Illinois in 1908, studied journalism there and in Missouri, roughed it during the Depression in New Mexico and as a fur trapper in subarctic Canada, married in Colorado, started writing in Santa Fe for the pulps, hit it big, moved to Aspen, wrote steadily there and (briefly) in Hollywood, wintered in Arizona, and—back in Aspen again—succumbed in 1975 to cancer.

The present study is the first book ever published on Luke Short. This is surprising, since he was and is uniformly praised by critics and buffs alike for his absorbing characterization, skillful plots, suspenseful pace, and—above all—lively authenticity. My first chapter places him in the tradition of Western fiction and then sketches his biography. Then I begin a critical consideration of his fifty-one novels. I have chosen, reluctantly, to ignore his short stories, for two reasons: they are generally unavailable today, except in dusty periodical stacks of big libraries (no selection of his short fiction has ever been published in book form); further, his novels, which are readily accessible, best illustrate his content and style. My second chapter surveys his novel production in such a way as to show his patterns and versatility. Chapter 3 discusses his use of the West and Southwest as setting. Chapter 4 parades his character types before the reader: heroes, lawmen, villains, and women. Chapter 5 attempts to relate Short's plot situations to aspects of myth and legend. Chapter 6 discusses nine of his interwoven themes and topics—justice, duty, chivalry, "bury the dead," self-awareness, joy's indirections, East versus West, "ends justify means," and the inefficacy of mob action. Chapters 7 and 8 analyze Short's literary style, and include a consideration of point of view and dialogue, methods of characterization, humor, structural devices, Short's unique lingo, and his stylistic infelicities and more importantly his undeniable charms. Chapter 9 is a terse recapitulation—brief because Luke Short is an action novelist whose value as an entertainer is obvious and whose excellences are almost so. It is my hope that this book, which was really fun to research and write, will send seasoned old Short addicts back to their easy chairs and recruit a million young new ones.

It is a pleasure to record my gratitude to a number of people who made this study possible and maybe also a little more accurate. Mrs. Frederick D. Glidden of Aspen, Colorado, and her son Daniel Glidden of nearby Basalt were most hospitable and informative, when I visited them, notebook in hand. In addition, Mrs. Glidden courteously answered innumerable nosy questions by mail. Dr. Edward Kemp and Ms. Deirdre Malarkey of the Library of the University of Oregon, at Eugene, Oregon, were cooperative and knowledgeable when they allowed me to read the Glidden Papers there. (I wish also to express my sense of obligation to the late Martin Schmitt, former curator of Special Collections at the University of Oregon Library.) I could have gone neither to Aspen nor on to Oregon if it had not been for a Faculty Research Grant from the Faculty of Arts and Sciences, University of Pittsburgh, and for the additional generosity of Dr. Mary Louise Briscoe, chairman of the Department of English, University of Pittsburgh; both provided much-appreciated funds for travel and related expenses. Professor Warren G. French, of Indiana University—Purdue University, Indianapolis, deserves special credit for prompt and expert supervision in his capacity as field editor for the Twayne's United States Authors Series volumes falling in the period of 1945 to the present. I am grateful also to Thomas T. Beeler, former executive editor of the Twayne Division and now publisher of G. K. Hall & Co., and the members of his exemplary staff, for their encouragement and efficiency. And I thank Steve Frazee, of Salida, Colorado, Brian Garfield, of Alpine, New Jersey, Dwight Newton, of Bend, Oregon, T. V. Olsen, of Rhinelander, Wisconsin, and H. N. Swanson, of Los Angeles, California—five professional associates and personal admirers of Fred Glidden—for generously sharing their knowledge and memories of an obviously inspiring, compassionate friend. Obtaining Luke Short paperback novels was a chore, and I thank the following for helping me corral them all: Ms. Pat Browne, Popular Press, Bowling Green, Ohio; Clarence W. Decater, Roseville, California; Dr. Linda DeLowry, Department of English, University of Pittsburgh; Edna's Book Exchange, Ashland, Oregon; Ms. Christine Gale, Pittsburgh; David L. Jenchura, Philadelphia; Alfred M. Slotnick, Brooklyn, New York; and the Unique Book Stall, Reno, Nevada. I am deeply grateful to Bantam Books, Dell Publishing Company, Inc., Fawcett Publications, Inc., and Mrs. Glidden, for permission to quote from copyrighted material. Finally, many thanks to my family for their love and steadying influence.

ROBERT L. GALE

University of Pittsburgh

Acknowledgments

Selections from *Ambush*, © 1948, 1949, 1976; *And the Wind Blows Free*, © 1943, 1945, 1970; *Coroner Creek*, © 1945, 1973; *Dead Freight for Piute*, © 1939, 1940, 1967; *Debt of Honor*, © 1967; *Desert Crossing*, © 1961; *The Deserters*, © 1969; *Donovan's Gun*, © 1968; *The Feud at Single Shot*, © 1935, 1963; *Fiddlefoot*, © 1946, 1973; *First Campaign*, © 1965; *First Claim*, © 1960; *Gunman's Chance*, © 1941, 1968; *The Guns of Hanging Lake*, © 1968; *Hard Money*, 1938, 1940, 1965; *Hardcase*, © 1941, 1942, 1970; *High Vermilion*, © 1947, 1974; *Last Hunt*, © 1962; *Man from the Desert*, © 1971; *The Man from Two Rivers*, © 1974; *The Outrider*, ©; *Paper Sheriff*, © 1966; *Play a Lone Hand*, © 1950; *The Primrose Try*, © 1967; *Raiders of the Rimrock*, © 1938, 1939, 1966; *Ramrod*, © 1943, 1971; *Ride the Man Down*, © 1942, 1969; *Rimrock*, © 1955; *Saddle by Starlight*, © 1952; *Silver Rock*, © 1953; *The Some-Day Country*, © 1963, 1964; *The Stalkers*, © 1973; *Station West*, © 1946, 1974; *Summer of the Smoke*, © 1958; *Sunset Graze*, © 1942, 1969; *Three for the Money*, © 1970; *Trouble Country*, © 1976; *Vengeance Valley*, © 1949, 1950, 1976; *War on the Cimarron*, © 1939, 1940, 1966; and *The Whip*, © 1956, 1957—quoted by permission of Bantam Books, Inc., and Mrs. Frederick D. Glidden.

Selections from *Bold Rider*, © 1938, 1966; *Bought with a Gun*, © 1940, 1967; *Bounty Guns*, © 1939, 1967; *Brand of Empire*, © 1937, 1965; *The Branded Man*, © 1936, 1963, 1964; *King Colt*, © 1937, 1964; *The Man on the Blue*, © 1936, 1937, 1964; *Marauders' Moon*, © 1937, 1964; *Raw Land*, © 1940, 1968; and *Savage Range*, © 1938, 1966—quoted by permission of Dell Publishing Co., Inc., and Mrs. Frederick D. Glidden.

Selections from *Barren Land Showdown*, © 1940, 1951, 1967—quoted by permission of Fawcett Publications, Inc., and Mrs. Frederick D. Glidden.

Selections from the unpublished letters of Frederick D. Glidden, deposited in the Library of the University of Oregon, Eugene, Oregon—quoted by permission of Mrs. Frederick D. Glidden.

Chronology

1908   Frederick Dilley Glidden ("Luke Short") born November 19 in Kewanee, Illinois, second of two sons of Wallace Dilley Glidden (died 1921) and Fannie Mae (Hurff) Glidden (died 1973); their other son: Jonathan H. ("Jon") Glidden ("Peter Dawson," 1907–57).

1926   Graduated from Kewanee High School and entered University of Illinois at Urbana.

1929   Transferred to University of Missouri at Columbia and graduated in 1930 with bachelor's degree in journalism.

1931–   Trapped furs in northern Alberta, Canada.
1933

1933   Worked as archaeologist's assistant in and near Santa Fe, New Mexico.

1934   June 18, married Florence Elder in Grand Junction, Colorado (three children: James, 1940–60; Kate [Hirson], 1941; Daniel, 1942); September, started writing fiction for pulp magazines, in Pojoaque, outside Santa Fe; November, began thirty-two-year association with New York literary agent Marguerite E. Harper.

1935   February, sold first short story; March, adopted Luke Short as pen name; August, published first novel, *The Feud at Single Shot*, in serial form.

1938   Enjoyed working vacation with wife in Scandinavia (February, March).

1940   Sold first idea to movies.

1941   March, *Saturday Evening Post* starts serializing *Blood on the Moon* (book title: *Gunman's Chance*), one of Short's top best-sellers; intermittently in Hollywood (July, until February 1942).

1942   April, *Saturday Evening Post* starts serializing *Ride the Man Down*, another of Short's top best-sellers.

1943   Again in Hollywood (January, April); November, took up residence in Washington, D.C., to work for Office of Strategic Services (until October 1944).

1944   October, returned to Santa Fe area.

1945   May, *Saturday Evening Post* starts serializing *Coroner Creek*, another of Short's top best-sellers; September, started lucrative relationship with paperback publishers.

1946   March, in Hollywood working on *Ramrod* movie script; December, began association with Bantam Books.

1947   August, moved to Aspen, Colorado; movie *Ramrod* released.

1948   Four Short novels produced as successful Hollywood movies: *Albuquerque* (based on *Dead Freight for Piute*), *Blood on the Moon* (based on *Gunman's Chance*), *Coroner Creek*, and *Station West*.

1951   March, began association with Dell Publishing Company.

1953   June, joined Western Writers of America.

1955   October, conferred with Lucille Ball and Desi Arnaz on television script-writing. Helped found thorium corporation in Colorado.

1956   June, negotiated with Bantam concerning original paperback novels; December, helped establish shortlived television-company partnership.

1958   Won Maggie award, Medallion of Merit, for *The Whip* (1956).

1960   April, son James Glidden accidentally drowned at Princeton, New Jersey.

1963   Vacationed and wrote in Virgin Islands (January–May); July, obtained more generous Bantam contract.

1964   Bought winter home in Wickenburg, Arizona.

1966   May, engaged H.N. Swanson of Los Angeles to be literary agent (Swanson had long been Short's movie-rights agent); June, donated papers to University of Oregon.

1969   Developed severe eye trouble; won Levi Strauss Western Writers of America award (Golden Saddleman award).

1974   Won Western Heritage Wrangler award; November, condition diagnosed as terminal throat cancer.

1975   Died August 18 at Aspen Valley Hospital, cremated, ashes buried at Aspen Grove Cemetery, Aspen, Colorado.

1976   February, fifty-first novel, *Trouble Country*, published.

1977   Luke Short memorial erected in Aspen Mall, Aspen, Colorado.

CHAPTER 1

Western Fiction and Luke Short

I N the beginning was the West. Much later came the Indians. After them came white explorers, then forest and prairie and mountain men, pioneers, and settlers, and—with these hordes— fighters of sundry sorts. Almost from the beginning of the exploitation of that never-Virgin Land came exploiters of a gentler sort: the writers.

I *Literary Context*

Among the first serious literary exploiters of the American West were eighteenth-century European Primitivists.[1] They began the process of mis-explaining the real Far West to genteel readers both in Europe and along the American Eastern seaboard.[2] This mis-education continued thanks to writers of the notorious dime novel,[3] the phenomenal success of which countered the culturally more significant and ultimately longer-lived writings of James Fenimore Cooper and Robert Montgomery Bird, among a few others, dealing with the West.[4] Quasi-documentary accounts of such now partially mythical figures out of Western history as Daniel Boone, Davy Crockett, Kit Carson, General George Armstrong Custer, and William F. "Buffalo Bill" Cody, not to mention Billy the Kid, Wild Bill Hickok, and Wyatt Earp,[5] also obscured better and more accurate literature of the West by such varied practitioners, for example, as Bret Harte, Mark Twain, and Theodore Roosevelt.

Meanwhile, shortly after the Civil War, the Far Western cattle industry sprang up. For our purposes, it was almost as though it had done so to infuse tired Western writing with new subject matter, and to thrill a reading public which should by then have grown sick of Deadwood Dick and even Calamity Jane. The new subject was the cowboy. The cowboy bossed cattle along trails,

17

and bossing the cowboy was the cattle baron, who was soon opposed not only by rivals of his own sort but also by the sheepman and then the homesteading farmer, who soon bought barbed wire.[6]

A friend of Teddy Roosevelt and the first genuinely meritorious writer of Westerns was Owen Wister. His novel *The Virginian* (1902) was, almost simultaneously, a superb novel, a challenging model to follow, and a misleading example.[7] It depicts an engagingly stalwart Western hero, seen and admired by an Eastern tenderfoot narrator, and judged adversely but then finally loved by a peppy heroine. It is episodic but suspenseful; and it shows the hero taking the law into his own hands according to the Western code, rationalizing lynch action, winning the girl, and changing with the Progressive times. So successfully did it establish certain Western stereotypes—hero, flawed friend, doomed enemy, folksy judge, schoolmarm, tall-tale humorist, racism, smoky poker game, and walkdown—that it both inspired and dominated competition, and delayed innovation as well.

The last word concerning the West, however, can never be said. So two types of words began—or rather continued—to be said by writers of Westerns immediately after *The Virginian*. Serious, capable literary figures such as Stewart Edward White, Andy Adams, Eugene Manlove Rhodes, and Bertha Sinclair ("B.M. Bower") outshone but undersold early twentieth-century pulp writers whose names (for example, W.C. Tuttle, Henry Herbert Knibbs, and William McLeod Raine) are now forgotten. Between several fine writers and dozens of inartistic pulpers stand such respectable figures as Clarence Mulford and Emerson Hough.[8]

What defense may be offered for the next big names? They are Zane Grey and Frederick Faust ("Max Brand"). Both wrote far too much and allegedly left enough finished material at their respective deaths to keep their publishers happily grinding out posthumous best-sellers in their names for years, nay, decades. Zane Grey's reputation among serious literary critics has fallen considerably; yet a distinguished defender of the popular arts in America has recently praised Grey for his appealing action, his use of "historical data," his "powerful sense of place," and even his introduction into the Western of occasional "mind-numbing [female] sensuality."[9] As for Max Brand, another fine critic cites him as the example par excellence of a writer whose production can be "spectacular . . . [as to] quantity," because he relies admirably on formulaic devices.[10]

Love of traditional Westerns continued unabated through the Roaring Twenties. But shortly after the Crash, the forces which had shaped the experimental writings of post-World War I America tried to make their impact on serious pulp and slick Western writers as well, and partially succeeded. From about 1930 or so, until the pervasive post-World War II disillusionment of young America caused by the Cold War and its tragic aftermath, the American Western frayed into separate strands which can never be woven together again. One critic has divided the post-1930 Western into three parts: artistically serious novels (for example, several by Conrad Richter, Frederick Manfred, and Walter Van Tilburg Clark), more formulaic pulp, and "the third strain . . . [which] lies somewhere between the multileveled symbolism of Clark and the specious commercialism of the production-line hack"[11]—that is, competent and sincere writers who, nevertheless, aim candidly for the avid mass market.

In this big group belong Ernest Haycox, Henry Wilson Allen ("Clay Fisher," "Will Henry"), Louis L'Amour, and Frederick Dilley Glidden ("Luke Short"), among several others. These men have provided honest entertainment not only to Middle America's innumerable escapist readers, many of them in T-shirt and armchair, with pipe, beer, and dog within handy reach, but also to even more numerous moviegoers and, especially in the 1950s, Western television addicts. In addition, consumers of such Westerns include professional men and women, housewives, sportsmen, jocks, teenagers, and assorted others.[12]

Such writers, some of whom could and still can turn out a Western of 50,000 to 65,000 words in two to six weeks, necessarily follow variations of an established, tried-and-true formula. It goes like this. Establish a clear sense of place and at least a general sense of time. Concentrate on your hero, give him a trusted friend, but don't stress the heroine and her sexiness too much. Choose a violent plot, wind it up to move in a hurry, and make the conflict between hero and double-dyed villain clear and basic. Such conflict can be underscored best when, as a leading pop-culture critic notes, "the point of encounter [is] between civilization and wilderness, East and West, settled society and lawless openness."[13] Use historical data but never obtrusively, since addicted readers prefer their own image of the Old West to any silly academic revisionist's truth.[14]

Next came the browning of America, disillusionment, and the antihero. Thomas Berger's *Little Big Man* (1964) and all that it is symptomatic of will not spell the doom of the traditional Western, but it surely hurts. And it seems apt that this novel appeared just before a fall in the ratings of the once-mighty television Western series, the discrediting of the Green Berets, and a general decline in American hero worship. Moreover, the formulaic Western is now in danger of ruin by the infusion of sadistic violence and kinky sex.[15]

Two highly competent Western writers whom Luke Short especially admired were Rhodes and Haycox. When Short was asked to provide biographical material for *Saturday Evening Post* publicity on the eve of its issuing his *Blood on the Moon* (later called *Gunman's Chance*), he replied with a typical minimum of words about himself but then added with characteristic modesty that he felt like ducking whenever people named him in the same breath with Gene Rhodes.[16] Later, Haycox was the subject of the only piece of literary criticism Short ever wrote. It dismisses Zane Grey in one terse clause and briefly praises Rhodes (and also *Saturday Evening Post* writer James Warner Bellah), but then positively rhapsodizes over Haycox for his masterly handling of hero, mood, place, dialogue, plot, and message, and for his combination of authenticity and "his own geography."[17] Imagine Short's joy upon receiving in 1941 a complimentary letter from Rhodes's widow, commending him as an able successor to her late husband, and also a pleasant letter from Haycox commending Short's fiction.[18]

II   *Frederick D. Glidden: Early Life*

There was a real Luke Short (1854-1893). He was a formidable, dapper little gambler, saloon keeper, and gunfighter in the environs of Dodge City, Kansas, well known for his fearless exploits and also such hairtrigger cronies as Bat Masterson, Doc Holliday, and Wyatt Earp, among others.[19] When Fred Glidden first tried to break into pulp print and decided to take a pen name which might sound more probable than his own, either he or his literary agent came up with "Luke Short."[20] Soon

Glidden's *nom de guerre* was more famous than the old gambler's real one.

Frederick Dilley Glidden was born on November 19, 1908, in Kewanee, Illinois, which is halfway between Peoria, Illinois, and Davenport, Iowa. Young Glidden's father was Wallace Dilley Glidden, who worked in a secretarial capacity for a local boiler company and who died in 1921. Glidden's mother was Fannie Mae (Hurff) Glidden, who, following her husband's death, taught English in Kewanee High School and still later became dean of women at Knox College, in nearby Galesburg, Illinois. She died in 1973. Glidden's older brother, Jonathan ("Jon") Glidden, born 1907, completed his high-school education in Kewanee and later distinguished himself as a minor writer of Westerns (under the pen name "Peter Dawson") until his death in 1957.

Young Fred Glidden was a typical high-school student and leader in Kewanee, doing well in his studies, going out for school activities, playing on the basketball and football teams, and being captain of the latter during his senior year, which was 1925–26.[21]

Next came two and a half years at the University of Illinois, at Urbana, where Glidden took a variety of courses, mostly in the humanities, for a variety of grades. Then, wanting to major in journalism and preferring a program elsewhere, he transferred in January 1929 to the distinguished School of Journalism at the University of Missouri, at Columbia, where he was awarded a bachelor's degree in June 1930.

The future Luke Short then alternately enjoyed and suffered through four years of wandering. As a press release put it much later, "Mr. Glidden worked on five middle western dailies as general reporter for extremely short periods. The bottom of the depression found him trapping in Canada. Because of the scarcity of jobs, newspaper or otherwise, he [then] turned to writing magazine fiction."[22]

Between the Canadian experience and the start of his literary career, two events of great importance to Glidden occurred. First, he moved to New Mexico and became an archaeologist's assistant, working at locating and mapping ruins in El Morro National Park. Second, still restless and anxious to capitalize on his growing familiarity with horses and cattle, Glidden persuaded a friend to go to Wyoming with him to find ranch work there. But in Greeley, Colorado, on the way north, Glidden met bright, lovely Florence Elder of Grand Junction at a sorority dance. Within weeks they were married—specifically on June 18, 1934—in Grand Junction and were soon on their way back to New Mexico, to the Pojoaque Valley outside Santa Fe, where they rented a house for $10 a month.[23]

Unemployment combined with reading of Western pulps led to Glidden's conclusion that he could write fiction at least as good as what he had been reading. So in September he started to try. His first tales, about Canadian trappers and Indians, generated only rejection slips, until a friend recommended that he write Marguerite E. Harper, a New York literary agent. He did so, and she began to advise him most cannily. In March 1935 he sent her his first book, signed Luke Short, in April she sent him $130 (less her 10 percent commission) for a wretched story she had peddled for him to Street & Smith, and in May he promised to double his monthly wordage to sixty thousand. Luke Short was launched.

Since Short wrote best about the West and the Southwest in the 1870s, 1880s, and 1890s, rarely cast his fiction in the twentieth century, and never successfully fictionalized aspects of his own life, it seems advisable to present the remainder of his biography in the barest of terms.

The last four years of Short's 1930s were marked by steady financial success. He averaged almost $800 a month, even though the United States had not yet worked itself out of the Depression.[24]

During the 1930s Short published fourteen novels, in addition to many short stories, usually undistinguished. In January 1938 he and his wife took a freighter out of Galveston, Texas, bound for Norway, planning a six-months' working vacation: Oslo until spring, then Finland into the summer. Things did not go well, however; so after sampling Scandinavia more briefly, they returned before mid-April.[25]

III   Short's Phenomenal 1940s

The 1940s provided Luke Short with his happiest, most stimulating years. In the first place, he and his charming wife had three children in three years. In addition, Short was smitten by the silver-screen bug (to be followed in due time by a secondary infection caused by the TV virus). Later in 1940 his agent, working in close cooperation with the distinguished Hollywood writers' agent H. N. Swanson of Sunset Boulevard, Los Angeles, sold a mediocre Short yarn entitled "Hurry, Charlie, Hurry" to RKO Radio Pictures for $1,000, allegedly for an incident to be wedged into a Blondie movie but converted instead into a 1941 "B" feature called *Hurry, Charlie, Hurry*, and starring then popular comedian Leon Errol.[26] Part of the time in 1941, 1942, and 1943, Short was in or near Hollywood, although little of note came of his script-writing labors there. Poor eyesight, which had caused him to wear glasses from his pre-teen years, kept him out of military service; but late in 1943 he began a one-year tour of duty with the Office of Strategic Services in Washington, D.C.

As his royalties sagged, so naturally did the commissions of his agent, the redoubtable Miss Harper. So she began to cajole Short, to remind him of her past efforts when he was down and nearly out, to wheedle, and to complain of Manhattan's wartime and indeed eternal problems. When he once wrote that he seemed temporarily out of ideas, she obligingly offered several. When he wrote of ennui at his desk, she urged him to regard his trade as resembling those of clerks, grocers, salesmen, railroad workers, and food producers, and to keep up his productivity. She often included tidbits of her ongoing theory of artistic creativity: it requires fast work, 9 to 5, not slow and irregular; Short's own best books, she added, came out in one-month bursts. Short stuck with Miss Harper because she was loyal, hard-working, and meticulous, had generally good critical-commercial taste, shrewdly developed his business contacts (including foreign ones), and was dedicated to her clients—of whom he evidently was the best.

Immediately after World War II, Short began to earn real money. First, he established a lucrative relationship with paperback publishers, notably Dell and Bantam, which were just beginning to flourish. Second, the years 1946–48 constituted his Hollywood peak time.

Early in 1946 he was in California helping with the movie script of his popular novel *Ramrod*. The film appeared the following year; it starred Joel McCrea and has justly earned enduring praise.[27] In 1948 alone, four Luke Short novels appeared as movies. They are *Albuquerque* (from *Dead Freight for Piute*, starring Randolph Scott), *Blood on the Moon* (starring Robert Mitchum and Barbara Bel Geddes[28]), *Coroner Creek* (from the novel of the same name and starring Randolph Scott), and *Station West* (from the novel of the same name and starring Dick Powell).

Short must have hoped that he was in for glittering millions from the celluloid capital. If so, he was mistaken. But in the midst of these solid material successes he and his wife made a decision which brought them more joy than Hollywood ever could. In the summer of 1947 they bought an ineffably charming old Victorian house in Aspen, Colorado. What homing instinct drew them to this unique area of untrammeled living, heady sports, quiet communing with nature, and internationally acclaimed cultural events is hard to say. In any event, Short quickly learned to love it for its manifold attractions, not the least of which for him were the skiing, fishing, hunting, and mountain scenery, not to mention that its history includes wild stories from the silver-mining days of yore. Nearby was Denver, with its richly stocked Public Library, in the Western History Department of which Short often did research to authenticate realistic details of his fiction.

As the 1940s drew to a close, Short could look upon his recent literary production with immense satisfaction. Among fourteen novels, at least the following stand out as still the real thing: *Gunman's Chance, Ride the Man Down, Ramrod, Coroner Creek, Station West, High Vermilion,* and *Vengeance Valley.*[29] But obviously what pleased Short the most was his leaving the pulps behind, as evidenced by his success with that slick of slicks, the *Saturday Evening Post,* which in the 1940s alone offered prebook, serial publication to nine of his novels. In the same busy decade, Short was chagrined, however, when the *Post* editors rejected *Hardcase, Sunset Graze* (which he himself pronounced a "stinker"[30]), and *And the Wind Blows Free.* All of these Miss Harper promptly saw into print elsewhere. In addition, the *Post* of the 1940s provided a slick outlet for "Top Hand" and "The Danger Hole," two of Short's best short stories.

So the 1940s were a banner decade for Short in almost every way. During this time, the big money for writers was in slick-magazine publication of action novels, then movie adaptations of them, not in their hardbound-book publication.[31]

IV   *Short's Unsettled 1950s*

The 1950s for Short were marked by uncertainties, discontent, and a kind of futile kicking against the restrictive role in which a welcome but almost fatal success was casting him. His production of Western novels fell off accordingly. He published only six, of which hardly half can be called excellent. In truth, only *Saddle by Starlight* and *The Whip* and perhaps *Rimrock* are exciting today.[32] No wonder Miss Harper's letters through this decade constitute an unmodulated litany of complaint, to which Short turned an alternately sympathetic, amused, and deaf ear.

The decade began badly. Early in 1950 a Dutch publishing firm allegedly pirated two of Short's books. Subsequent attempts at international legal action proved costly, slow, and fruitless.[33] Later the same year, the *Post* rejected *Play a Lone Hand,* which Miss Harper promptly sold to *Collier's* for serial publication.[34] The next year was more auspicious: Short's Hollywood agent, H. N. Swanson, closed deals for the movie rights to *High Vermilion* and *Ride the Man Down.*[35] All the same, Short wanted different pastures, if not greener ones. So he and an Aspen friend named Joe Marsala early in 1952 composed the lyrics and music, respectively, for a musical comedy called *I've Had It,* in which a pair of unemployed Texas cowboys harmlessly spoof the long-haired aestheticism of summer Aspenites. The show enjoyed a few amateur performances, not only in Aspen but also in Denver; and Short thought well enough of it to secure its copyright. However, he and his collaborator were frustrated in their efforts to move its undoubted charms to Broadway.[36]

For nonartistic enlivenment, September 1952 brought evidence not of further literary piracy but of plagiarism from some of Short's novels by an unscrupulous American living in England and publishing fast there. As with the earlier piracy case and also several later plagiarism incidents, nothing either punitive or rewarding eventuated.[37] In the summer of 1953 Short flew to the Yellow Knife region north of Alberta, Canada, for on-the-spot observation of uranium mining and alleged Communist-inspired labor unionizing thereabouts. It was the belief of a new editor at *Collier's,* which meanwhile had accepted Short's *Saddle by Starlight* and *Silver Rock,* that fiction with contemporary punch might result. However, although Short drafted several versions of a story to be called "The Passenger," all efforts came to naught. All the same, early the following year he visited a Utah uranium mine in the company of a multi-millionaire, to add to his already considerable knowledge of radioactive minerals and to pick up local color of allied sorts, for his next novel, *Rimrock,* his strongest work in a contemporary setting.[38] At about this time, Short also participated in founding a thorium company in Aspen.

The year 1955 was especially agitated for Short. His thorium venture proved fruitless and shortlived. Although Bantam reported accumulated Short sales to the tune of 7 million, this knowledge only made his agent discontent with the royalty schedule established by Bantam, which she badgered unremittingly until she improved it.[39] In September Short developed an ill-starred hankering to coauthor, with a local airplane pilot, a handbook on how to fly over mountainous terrain.[40] The following month found Short briefly consorting with Desi Arnaz and Lucille Ball in Los Angeles. Short's later efforts to channel his one undeniable literary talent, for creating action-packed Westerns, into script-writing for television, if temporarily gratifying, soon enough also turned sour.[41]

It is clear from his correspondence at this time with his New York agent not only that writing Western novels was beginning to weary Short, but also that he was increasingly dissatisfied with his California business associates and their seeming inability to sell more of his fiction to the movies. He could not know then what we do now: after his Hollywood banner years of 1948–52, only two more works of his would be made into movies. They are *Silver Rock*, which became *Hell's Outpost*, and a short story entitled "The Hangman," which became a movie of the same name in 1959.[42]

The 1950s after this point saw only *Summer of the Smoke* come from Short's novelistic pen. It was rejected first by the *Saturday Evening Post* as unengaging and without enough sunshine[43] and thereafter by other periodicals as well. It has, therefore, the distinction of being Short's first Bantam original. Making a virtue of necessity, the Bantam ballyhooers boasted on its cover, "First time published anywhere!"

By way of nonartistic endeavor, Short became active as a member of the Aspen town council in the 1950s. He is still revered by Aspenites for his selfless devotion to hospital-administration reform, conservative tough-mindedness with respect to zoning, keeping neon lights and billboards far out of town, and preventing the rechanneling of his beloved Hunter Creek to the north.[44]

V   *Short's Dark 1960s*

As Short approached later middle age, he inevitably became reconciled to the twin facts that he was a splendid writer only of old-fashioned Westerns and that he would never be a big-time success in Hollywood. But the dream died hard. Meanwhile, partly because of the moderate popularity of Bantam editions of *First Claim, Desert Crossing,* and *Last Hunt,* Short returned to writing Westerns full time.

But for years after the onset of the 1960s, his heart could not have been in the work. The greatest personal tragedy of his life occurred when his son James accidentally drowned at the Princeton University swimming pool in April 1960. As Short wrote in *First Claim,* "It was the saddest part of life, that a father should see his son dead before him. . ." (p. 147).[45] His agent's boast to a Brazilian publisher seeking rights to reprint Short south of the Equator that her famous author's total sales exceeded 25 million by March 1962[46] could hardly have represented any consolation to the saddened author. After *Desert Crossing* and *Last Hunt,* he wrote *The Some-Day Country,* which, far from auguring an upswing in quality, is instead his weakest novel.

Next, Short decided not merely to try a totally new literary *donnée* but also to write it out while vacationing in a totally different environment. He and his wife spent several months early in 1963 at Christiansted, St. Croix, in the Virgin Islands, where he composed *Pearley.* This is a *Cannery Row*-like novel about an aging alcoholic and his war against a pipe-laying company in a little town much like Aspen and also about a salty woman who is grotesquely anxious for motherhood. The effort got nowhere, and only the non-Steinbeckian author saw merit in it.[47]

So Short was more than agreeable when Miss Harper negotiated a generous new contract with Bantam,[48] and he soon settled into what would become his professional routine for the remainder of his life. In 1964 he and his wife began their pattern of winter-vacationing in Arizona. A little later, they bought a second home there, in Wickenburg, about fifty miles northwest of Phoenix. By getting away to Arizona, they avoided the less and less appealing winter months in Colorado—with its cold, snow, wet, skiers, and mushrooming condominiums, which Short later called "Aspen Hong Kong."[49]

In 1964 Short hit upon the idea of centering several novels in the same town, which he called Primrose. This town initially appears in *First Campaign,* which followed his weak *Some-Day Country* and is one of his longest, strongest books. He planned at one point to make it even more raw by virtue of a near-rape scene.[50] By this time, Short thoroughly knew Aspen, a kind of partial model of Primrose. He had a big third-floor corner office in the Elks Building there, where he did most of his writing. While dictating fiction to a secretary, he could gander down on friends below, and, as he once put it, notice the increasing baldnesses and pregnancies thereof.[51]

Six more Short novels round out the 1960s. All are very fine. Half first appeared in the *New York Daily News;* then all were published by Bantam. But the seemingly indefatigable Marguerite Harper did not negotiate details for these works, most of which have action in or near Primrose, because by the summer of 1965 she was seriously sick. She died the following spring, shortly after wrapping up her files of correspondence with Short and shipping them out to him in Aspen for safekeeping.

Only one other event of the 1960s merits comment. In 1969 Short received the Levi Strauss Western Writers of America award, with its bronze statuette of a cowboy flourishing a branding iron which clearly reads "LS." Normally, the initials stand for Levi Strauss. But did Luke Short crack his typically infectious grin when he first saw the letters? I hope so.

VI   *The 1970s*

The 1970s saw the appearance of Short's last half-dozen novels. The first two have a distinctly comic tone, typically deadly though much of their action is. The final quartet, which constitute what we might now call Short's *ave atque vale,* revert autumnally to vintage Gliddenian violence. They were written under severe physical handicaps. In 1969 Short developed debilitating eye trouble. Never strong, his eyesight grew weaker. A cataract in his left eye worsened. Surgery did not correct it but instead was followed by a detached retina. Further surgery hindered instead of helping. All the same, he continued to write, alternating his habitual dictation with the use of legal-sized yellow tablets, which he filled with his fast, legible hand in soft pencil.

In 1974, Short was gladdened when he won the Western Heritage Wrangler award, but he was too sick to attend the colorful ceremonies at the National Cowboy Hall of Fame and Western Heritage Center, in Oklahoma City. By this time fate had struck him again, this time below his eyes and ready grin. He now had terminal throat cancer, which grew worse over a period of months. He endured radiation treatment and chemotherapy in Denver, but wasted away until his weight was little more than half his normal 160 lean-framed pounds. In the early morning of August 18, 1975, Frederick Dilley Glidden died in Aspen Valley Hospital. Soon thereafter his ashes were interred in Aspen Grove Cemetery, in the soil of a state he not only loved for its scenic beauty, vivid history, and fine people, but also memorialized in fiction often cast there.

CHAPTER 2

Survey of Luke Short's Novels

THE best way to obtain a notion of the range, depth, and formulaic quality of Luke Short's fiction may be to review his fifty-one novels in such a way as to see their salient features swiftly, even superficially.

I   The 1930s

In the 1930s Short published fourteen novels, beginning with *The Feud at Single Shot* (1936). In this book he establishes a basic pattern: the ill-used hero (Dave Turner here) with a shady but not disgusting past relies on a few trusted friends (including an old-timer) in his fight to retain his ranch from villains who want it for its gold. The town of Single Shot is typically shabby. One villain is gigantic and sadistic (he tortures Dave by nailing his hand to a table); the hidden power behind him, however, is even more dangerous. The law is honest but slow, out of touch, and usually ineffective. Contrasting heroines are the hero's sister, whose husband is a weak, Eastern city type and hence doomed, and Dorsey Hammond, the beautiful daughter of a mine operator falsely suspected. The novel has a lightning-fast but confusing first chapter. The book also has a typically troublesome title (there is no feud, and much action is out of town) and an ending which is almost undeviatingly typical of Short: evil is destroyed, and a late kiss signals a predictable proposal of marriage.

The Branded Man (also 1936) turns from fighting over gold to stealing cattle. The mission of the hero, Mark Flood, is to clear his family name, since his dead brother has been falsely branded as a rustler. On his road to success, Mark encounters mysterious Margot Curtin, who is a hotel worker in Clearcreek (with her doomed brother, Lee) and who is engaged to Loosh Petrie, a graceless, battered villain. Loosh of the Wagon Hammer spread is the rival of Bar Stirrup owner Ben Hand. Neither the local marshal nor the local sheriff seems able to intervene, either to prevent bloodshed or to keep Mark out. The hero tracks epically here.

The Man on the Blue (also 1936) introduces a new type of hero. He is Shamrock Ireland, described as "not tall, not heavy, either, but close-knit," with "rain-gray" eyes and an "arrogance [which] was regal" (p. 6) and able to perform feats of daring which make him legendary. Fleeing south out of Montana from a false charge of murder,[1] he rides his faithful blue into a murderous squabble over land between a lazy-looking sheriff tardily revealed as crooked and the Diamond D owner, who needs Shamrock's feisty help and who also has a gutsy sister.

Maurauders' Moon (1937) combines elements from *The Branded Man* and *The Man on the Blue*. Its hero, broad-shouldered, red-haired Webb Cousins, rides into a vicious war between rival ranchers, is suspected by inept lawmen, and soon persuades Martha, the daughter of good Buck Tolleston, to see the villainy of her fiancé, Britt, the son of evil Wake Bannister. Arson, a vivid feature of this novel, will become common in Short's later plots. One would be hard put to complete a body count here. (Close to thirty?) But it would have to include both a born loser who sees the futility of trying to escape and, therefore, rides purposely into a hail of lead and also a villainous gunman who eerily approaches his own death with a yawn.

King Colt (also 1937) was a step backward for Short. Too weak to merit many words, it features a fool who stages his own apparent death to shake his irresponsible foster son, the hero, into maturity. The conflict is over gold-bearing land in New Mexico. Short offers in Major Fitz the first of several martinet villains and in waitress Nora Jenkins a typical heroine who patiently waits for her man to prove himself with guns and fists before he can expect rewards from her.

Brand of Empire (also 1937) is marred by a confusing first section only partly redressed by flashbacks. It is livened by the most violence since *The Feud at Single Shot*. One victim's head, we read, "resembled the shell of a hard-boiled egg which has been dropped and rolled. The only thing holding it together was the scalp" (pp. 7–8). The man was a sadist and deserved his gory end, surely, because he had cut off the noses of two of hero Pete Yard's sisters. All the same, the dead man's brother, Ben Mellish, wants revenge as he happily works for master villain Senator Matthew Waranrode,[2] empire builder and exploiter of Western coal lands. A new plot element first employed here but common later is the attempt by the hero to organize divisive little nesters into a unit capable of resisting the villains. The law is so ineffective that the sheriff of Ten Troughs submits to his own kidnapping to help the good side. New character types include a crusading newspaper man, a well-read physician, and the hero's reliable Indian friend Stumbling Bear, a Ute subchief whose people are victimized by corrupt white bureaucrats.

The titular hero of *Bold Rider* (1938) is Poco St. Vrain. Like Shamrock Ireland, he is fabulously capable—whether he is outrunning the bumbling army, falling off cliffs, triple-crossing mutually double-crossing villains, rescuing the ashen-haired heroine, accepting the aid of a marshal named Sam Vanwolken-diefendorfer, or merely returning filched gold.

Savage Range (also 1938) fails to offer much that is new. In it, a land-hungry villain named Max Bonsell, with the passive connivance of a weak lawman, is systematically driving off a group of nesters, who are divided by guilt because of a murder long ago. Max hires good Jim Wade to be his ramrod, in order to make him his fall guy. Wade soon sees the truth, shifts allegiance, and aids romantic Mary Buckner, the rightful heiress to the vast Ulibarri land grant. She has been carefully kept under wraps by Jack Cope, an enormous, crippled saloon owner, until a hero such as Wade might come along. Crossed battle lines and incredible violence blur this unexceptional novel. One new touch, later overused, is the Gothic plot device of a missing deed.

The plot of *Raiders of the Rimrock* (also 1938) is even more tangled. Tim Enever intervenes, as a range detective summoned by a lawman soon stabbed to death, between villainous sheepman Warner Sands and the more established cattlemen led by old Jeff Hardy (owner of the Ox-Bow ranch). On his side is the heroine Martha Kincaid.[3] Tim's tasks are to organize the opposition to Sands, to bring to justice the lawman's killer, and to keep from harm not only Martha but also Sands's zombielike daughter Julie, before whose very eyes her villainous father is shot down by Tim, with the psychological assistance of a well-depicted gunman once in Sands's employ but then repentant. A new feature here is the kidnapping of a woman (to be repeated later).

Bounty Guns (1939) is mainly notable for its ingenious plot. In it, a murderer named Rig Holman hires unemployed rancher Tip Woodring to identify a killer. But the killer is Rig himself. His purpose is to have the hero fan the embers of the Shields–Bolling feud in and about the scummy town of Hagen, so that after the blood dries Rig can step in. He knows of gold in the region and wants to jump the secret claim of the man he killed. Predictably, a good Shields (named Buck) is in love with a good Bolling (named Anna). Less predictably, the dead miner's daughter is loitering in town under an assumed name, temporarily working in a newspaper office. She hopes for revenge, somehow, and is thus handy when Tip arrives. A brilliant little feature of this undistinguished novel is old Dave Shawn, who in the fourth chapter identifies for Tip every significant good man and every dangerous bad one. The briefing resembles a Shakespearean prophecy and adds to the charm of the plot's unfolding.

Hard Money (also 1939) is first-rate throughout, the best Short novel to its date.[4] The opening chapters, which vividly present the booming mine town of Tronah, are worthy of Willa Cather or Conrad Richter. Old Charles Bonal has made a fortune and is now fighting Servel Janeece, head of the General Milling and Mining Company, to preserve and extend it. So he cleans out tough gambler-engineer Phil Seay at faro and then hires him to boss his mining crew. The area marshal is ineffective. The local judge scurries out of town when he might be useful to Tronah's law-and-order advocates. Bonal's daughter Sharon, though beautiful, is spoiled and, furthermore, is engaged to a smooth man employed by her father but secretly in the villain's pay. Hence it seems actually possible that the hero may prefer to Sharon the captivating Vannie Shore, sexy, rich ex-mistress of a now dead mine owner. Overt villainy in the form of harshly named Chris Feldhake offers Phil many challenges—in poker, with fists, down watery mine shafts, and finally in the open street. In every way, this novel is superior, and its tender-tough hero is one of Short's best.

With *War on the Cimarron* (also 1939), Short takes a long step back. Frank Christian's motive is revenge: his partner has been murdered on the cattle trail, near Fort Reno and the town of Darlington—locales which will be prominent later in Short. We are initially unsure whether the guilty party is a beef and illegal whiskey supplier to the Cheyenne along the Cimarron, or

Frank's rival cattleman. In his quest for rough justice, the hero has considerable help, some from rather pacific members of his crew, but more from the gauche heroine Luvie Barnes, daughter of a local feed and livery man. Short uses a familiar plot feature when he has Frank cause wagon-wrecking, arson, and stampedes in such a way as to pit the two villains against each other.

Dead Freight for Piute (also 1939) is one of Short's finest books.[5] In it, Cole Armin, ruined young Texas rancher, reports to his freight-hauling "uncle" Craig Armin, who controls most of the business in the mining areas around Piute (near California) but wants it all. His embattled rival is young Ted Wallace, whose sister provides the love interest, especially after Cole switches sides upon learning that his "uncle" uses robbery, arson, and sabotage to weaken the Wallaces. Villains include the sheriff, his murderous henchman, and even sweet Letty Burns—who is misguided into blaming the wrong side for her brother's earlier death. Suspense is achieved when we see but do not know the cause of a sequence of vicious acts. The expert weaving into the story of mining details shows that Luke Short wrote only of what he knew.

Short's production of the 1930s was rounded off weakly by *Bought with a Gun* (also 1939), in which yet another legendary little escape artist, this one named Sam Teacher, is framed by yet another coarse villain. The rather silly plot takes on the contours of a chess game as the two adversaries tip their hands, gambit, and attack, almost as though the outcome were of less importance than the manner in which they show off. Sam's mission is to secure a land grant from a tired old rancher for the railroad friends of a governmental commissioner, who in return will clear up Sam's falsely tarnished name. The hero knights his way through perilous opposition, with the help of an "immaculate friend," in Herman Melville's sense. The cast includes two women: the old rancher's spoiled daughter and also the first of several tough businesswomen to appear in Short.

II   *The 1940s*

In the 1940s Short published thirteen novels and widened his range substantively and stylistically. *Barren Land Showdown* (1940) is the first of four Short novels having contemporary Western settings. In fact, to make it even more current, the publishers revised it for book publication in 1951 and interpolated a few inept Korean War references.[6] This novel is unique in having a Canadian setting—so effectively rendered that more fiction by Short with the same background would have been welcome. Unusual also is the fact that in this novel the representative of the law is totally admirable. Corporal Millis of the Royal Canadian Mounted Police is shrewd, tolerant, and willing to stretch a point to help the oppressed loner hero, Frank Nearing. Trying to take over an abandoned mining claim, Frank for needed money agrees to hide a man who says he is running from his wife but who is really a German saboteur. The novel is weakened by poorly managed mumbo-jumbo about strychnine in the coffee and dogfood, a simple-minded if sexy waitress, and an axe murder with a Gothic-ice background.

Raw Land (also 1940) offers a combination of several old ingredients and a few new elements. Becky is the good daughter of Angus Case, a retired rustler and killer who is repentant but still successful. Will Danning, the hero, returns to the region, where he formerly was a ranch hand for Angus, in order to buy Pitchfork, a scrubby spread in the brakes. He does so to hide his supposed friend Milton "Milt" Barron, who is on the run from a murder charge. Will does not know that Pitchfork is rich in copper. But Pres Milo, who is blackmailing Angus, knows. Further, Mary Norman knows who Milt really is (a murderer named Murray Broome), follows him, and is sexually inflamed by him. Complicating and ultimately dulling the tangled plot is tedious paper evidence in the form of a missing ranch deed, and also stolen and forged letters.[7]

Gunman's Chance (1941) is a big novel by Luke Short which should enjoy a long popularity.[8] It is one of his finest, most representative efforts, a splendid piece of action fiction. In it, Jim Garry is trying to distance himself from a shameful past. So when he reports for work to his former unsavory associate Tate Riling and sees the kind of villainy now being planned—forcing John Lufton to sell his cattle herd for a fraction of their worth to Riling, who intends to resell it to a crooked Indian agent—Jim shifts allegiance. He does so partly because of Lufton's two intriguing daughters. Amy is tough, quietly sexy, spunky, and attractive; but of her domineering sister Carol, doomed by her wild passion for Riling, we read:

. . . This was a woman who knew she was beautiful. Everything about her told him [Jim] so—the cut and the stuff of her dress, which was a strange green color that matched her eyes, the searching arrogant stare that summed him up, judged and dismissed him. . . . Her auburn hair, thick and silky and alive as light, had been pinned up off her neck in back. She had that drowsy and impatient look about her of a bored woman who has been waked from sleep only to be bored again. (pp. 15-16)

Short manages time in this novel with special care and cleverness: as the beef-sale deadline[9] approaches, time is running out for the hero, who, however, has made his final commitment and cannot be dissuaded from his course of violent action.

Hardcase (also 1941), contrariwise, offers little evidence of development in Short. In it, Dave Coyle, a minor little outlaw with a big reputation, helps an endangered rancher whose daughter only tardily changes her opinion and begins to respect the loner hero—for his courage, escapist prowess, and even courtroom ability. Mechanical plot devices such as a forged bill of sale and a receipt for a bribe signed by the villain weaken the book, which is, however, livened by Short's first dramatic court scene.

With *Ride the Man Down* (1942), Short recovered impressively. It presents little that is new, but it is solid and absorbing. Will Ballard is foreman of Hatchet ranch, once run well by Phil Evarts, upon whose death his brother John can neither keep rival neighbor Bide Marriner from encroaching nor persuade an underhanded neighbor, engaged to dead John's daughter, to make a stand against Bide. Will's teacher girl friend wishes that there might be less violence, since it is immoral and also is bad for her merchant father's business; but the reader cannot endorse her strictures.

Sunset Graze (also 1942) turns on the hero Dave Wallace's desire to investigate the suspicious death of a friend, features a heroine named Beth Hilliard who made the mistake of leaving her ranch property in the hands of a supposed old friend while she spent a year or two back East, includes a tall old villain who has a disarming "thick ruff of dead-white hair" (p. 3) and who is evidently turns evil after becoming " 'damn sick of being sweet and kind and nice. . .' " (p. 150), and adds a colorful old wolfer named Ives. A new form of plot complication is the honest but inept sheriff's dog-in-the-manger love for Beth. A thematic innovation is the fatalistic attitude toward death evinced by the intrepid hero.

And the Wind Blows Free (1943) begins brilliantly, has complexities enough for a very long novel, but limps a little to its slightly premature end. It introduces three new elements in Short: young Joel Hardy tells the story in the first person; his idol Jim Wade (no relation to hero Jim Wade of *Savage Range*) is in love with a married woman (the combination of these two elements—young narrator and illicit love—gives the novel something of the tone of *A Lost Lady* by Willa Cather); and seven real-life personages are mentioned or alluded to.[10] The action takes place partly around Fort Reno and Darlington; moreover, the son of Stone Bull, a violent Indian who appeared briefly in *Gunman's Chance*, figures briefly in the action here. Fascinatingly described are two contrasting calamities: a prairie fire and a blizzard.

Short followed this experimental novel with *Ramrod* (also 1943), one of his finest works. Its special appeal, like that of *Gunman's Chance*, lies in the self-regeneration of the hero, in this case through his search for something to be loyal to after the death of his wife and child. Dave Nash wanders into the town of Signal, is befriended there by a local dressmaker named Rose Leland, hires on as foreman at arrogantly beautiful little Connie Dickason's Circle 66 ranch, and quickly clashes with Frank Ivey, a vicious thug who owns the nearby Bell ranch and wants more range land. To buy time for embattled Dave, his flawed friend Bill Schell memorably sacrifices himself and thus prepares for the wild conclusion. Along the way are introduced a wistful teen-aged ranch hand, a middle-aged woman who hides the wounded hero in her bedroom and scares off the pursuers while in a state of unattractive undress, and a lawman who is over the hill but is armed with a "wintry chill" (p. 3) which never falters.

Next came another Short classic—*Coroner Creek* (1946). Chris Danning has tracked and now located Younger Miles, who helped the villainous Indian Tana butcher a wagon train, then took the gold being shipped on it. Chris's fiancée was killed, as were all the other whites. Miles is now a successful, ruthless rancher, near the town of Triumph. Chris hires on as ramrod at a rival spread owned by a widow and her timorously appealing daughter, exploits the temporary alcoholism of Miles's unhappy wife, daughter of the scared sheriff, and soon becomes involved in terrifying varieties of violence. Love interest is provided by yet another woman, who runs a hotel in town and has a pleasant, crippled father.

Nothing very complimentary can be said for the popular *Fiddlefoot* (also 1946), in which an only moderately engaging hero named Frank Chess too rapidly changes for the better as he attempts to outgrow his generally deserved label of worthlessness, and too slowly sees both the prissiness of his fiancée, Carrie Tavister, and also the attractiveness of Tess Falette. Tess may live by herself, work as an accountant for the enormous villain, and play poker in her spare time; but she is incomparably peppier than immature Carrie. The novel is weakened by the fact that its action is frequently caused by others rather than being initiated by the hero.

Station West (also 1946), on the other hand, is one of Short's masterpieces. It features Lieutenant John Sargent Haven, his first military hero, although he poses as a civilian and a criminal. He must worm his way into the confidences of those suspected of stealing army uniforms in order to dress their ruffians in them for a raid against depleted Fort Stambaugh and its stored gold. So Haven swaggers into nearby South Pass City and beats up huge Mick Marion, the toughest man in town and the master-villain's partner in crime. Haven soon becomes an almost trusted member of the gang. Credible detective work by the hero leads, through a thicket of plot complications, to an agreeable, noisy climax.[11]

High Vermilion (1947) returns to a mining region like those in a few earlier novels, and again Short paints a realistic locale as backdrop for brutal action. And here again we have a hero with a flawed past. He is engineer-assayer Larkin Moffat, who once took a bribe to fake an assay report—all for money to win a beautiful but corrupt girl he later spurned in revulsion. He then escaped farther west; but he finds that he cannot forever avoid either his conscience or gorgeous Josephine, who is now married to villainous Charlie Storrs. So Larkin admits his misdeed to potential scorners and pounds them if they try to taunt him. A bloated, greedy mine owner bent on extending his claims, and backed by violent guns, opposes the hero and his good employer, who has an attractive daughter. From the outset, the town of Vermilion, which is aptly called "a whiskey camp, not a champagne one" (p. 7), is almost a character.[12]

Ambush (1948) turns again to military action. This time the hero, army scout Ward Kinsman, is without blemish and in addition offers the Eastern heroine a well-articulated philosophy of life, which includes praise of the way of life of the Apaches whom he is hired and destined to oppose and supplant. The ineptly led American army unit's mission in New Mexico territory is to find and free a white woman held by renegade Apache Diablito and his divided cohorts. The plot is excellently complicated by a likable officer's love for a murderous, drunken Irish enlisted man's attractive but high-minded laundress wife, and by a skillful dramatization of the loneliness of command. *Ambush* would be first-rate but for certain plot meanderings, too much action occurring offstage, and the absence of any villain. Two interesting touches: the hero is knocked flat in a fistfight with a supercilious military officer, and Tana from *Coroner Creek* reappears here.

Vengeance Valley (1949), which rounds off Short's production in the 1940s, explores the question of loyalty. Is the stubborn, fierce hero Owen Daybright disloyal to himself when he loyally hides the identity of the father of unwed Lily Fasken's baby from her vengeful hillbilly brothers and lets them think he is the culprit? Is he loyal to beautiful and neighborly Jen Canafax when he thus jeopardizes his own safety? Is loyalty carried too far when, in return for having been adopted by old Arch Stobie, Owen is kind to Arch's son Lee, who is Lily's feckless married lover?

III   *The 1950s*

In the 1950s Luke Short's production of novels fell off in quantity. *Play a Lone Hand* (1950) is not outstanding but does have one memorably chilling sequence. It presents yet another repentant, canny gunman hero, and yet another vicious, empire-building range ruler. Giff Dixon, a reformed would-be bank robber, takes a job as a surveyor's assistant, declines to support the dishonesty of his pusillanimous, alcoholic boss, and survives numerous attacks to lure the villain into unforgettable ruina-tion—by diverting a hired killer from his original object to the hirer himself.

Saddle by Starlight (1952) again features the disengagement of whilom lovers. They are loyal foreman-hero Sam Holley and unstable Virginia Talcott, who foolishly thinks that a crooked government surveyor named Hugh Ganley can bring her happiness. Sam leads a group of small ranchers, varyingly honest but increasingly in disarray, against nesters hired by Hugh to homestead so that he can grab the land. But then Sam falls in love with Julia Rainey, sister of one of the rousted nesters, gets her a job with a rancher who turns out to be vicious but whose wife is a veritable saint, and has more and more trouble with gunnies hired by Hugh, and even with some of his neighbors. Straining for new forms of homicide, Short seizes upon death by brickbat. One of the finest things about this admirable novel is its haunting title.[13]

With *Silver Rock* (1953) Short explodes violent action against another contemporary backdrop—in this instance making his flawed hero an injured Marine Corps pilot back from the Korean War. Tully Gibbs learned from his radarman, now dead, of a zinc, lead, and silver mine in Azurite,[14] owned by the dead airman's father but incapable of being developed because of corrupt county commissioners. References to martinis and the composer Béla Bartók jar most Western buffs' insensibilities here, and in other ways this effort is not one of the author's best. Tully is simply not a pleasant hero.

The action of *Rimrock* (1955) is also in modern dress. But this time the uranium-seeking hero Dave Borthen's characterization is credible; and when his unliberated girl friend quits her safe job and sneakily takes a typing assignment in the field office of Holly Heath, Short's first and most venomous villainess, all readers applaud. For plot balance, Dave has a traitor in his camp as well. Further, to match his loyal old friend Hutch Elden, Holly is aided by a pugnacious bodyguard, a former Reno cop named Chief Buford. Ute City, Colorado, and the desert area near Joash, Utah, to the west, are especially well rendered. This is Short's best tale of twentieth-century adventure.

The Whip (1956) is Short's briefest novel and one of his most fascinating. It concerns yet another hero with a troubled background. Here, Will Gannon, formerly a stage-line manager, quits, travels east, and tries by mindless escapism to forget his adulterous wife until he encounters a company branch line murderously mismanaged by Lou Meydet, head of a virulent gang. Lou meets his match in Will, whose arsenal includes mayhem, driving his friends to exhaustion, steady guns, and even lynching.[15] Four curious women appear in *The Whip:* the Indian squaw of a sensual friend of Will's named Hutch Forney (i.e., fornicator?), a dirty inn-manager's hoydenish daughter, a nerveless old housekeeper, and redoubtable Carrie Bentall. Carrie is orphaned, has Eastern prejudices against violence, is the most courageous Short heroine, and is torn—as Will himself is—between personal beliefs and love.

Summer of the Smoke (1958) rounds off the decade of the 1950s for Short, who here presents as his hero another unappreciated army scout, another Apache renegade, another loyal laundress (though single this time), and more bumbling military leaders—all staples from his better *Ambush*. Old Tana is even mentioned again. But a new type of character is first presented here—the villain's slatternly wife, who is tense and sadly wise—along with a new emblem of violence, a severed white arm sent back to the little Southwestern town by redskins as a graphic warning. Violence soon mounts: if my casualty figures are accurate, the villain is the thirteenth of seventeen varmits to die by the penultimate page.

IV   *The 1960s*

In the 1960s eleven Luke Short novels appeared, several of them excellent, but one — *The Some-Day Country*—his weakest. *First Claim* (1960) has an interesting *donnée* which is, however, not worked out well, since the hero is reluctant to be ultimately violent in his own cause. Giff Ballew leaves Wyoming to claim his father's stolen land near Harmony, New Mexico, in 1879. The young heroine, a widowed newspaper worker, dislikes trouble; and so does the villainous old land grabber's younger son, Lee Waybright. But Lee's tough, immoral brother Tucker thrives on it. Unlikely evidence in the form of a torn neckerchief and a missing deed, not to mention two or three hairbreadth escapes by Giff when he is wounded, strains credibility; and the climax is thematically unsatisfactory.

In *Desert Crossing* (1961), Short stars Dave Harmon, an ex-army officer with an eye patch and a steely resolve to make a success of his freighting business. When he agrees to haul thirty crates of rifles from California across the Mohave Desert to Fort Whipple, Arizona, he is severely challenged; opposing him are two vicious white outlaws and their men (who want to steal the rifles), Apaches mostly over the horizon, and even a whining

Eastern businessman along for the ride part of the way. Neither a small army escort for Dave nor a separate military party under a ridiculous martinet making an independent sweep nearby can provide Dave the help he should have. Short excellently sketches coastal and inland freighting niceties, while an attractive heroine is unique in having two living parents, awaiting her at the fort on ahead.[16]

Last Hunt (1962), cast in post-Korean War times, is Short's final novel with a contemporary setting. The detective ingenuity of Lee McPhail, a game-and-fish officer out of Ute City, is tested when his surrogate father, a distinguished lawyer and judge, is found murdered while on a little hunting trip. A depraved killer, a suspected bigamist, a pair of women disreputable in different ways, and a pair of unsatisfactory law officers comprise only part of the large cast of characters of this somewhat confusing story.[17] The victim's attractive secretary, who is Lee's fiancée but was also once the object of the sheriff's desires, is almost worthy of her hero.

The Some-Day Country (1963), Short's least effective novel, concerns illegal immigrants and would-be homesteaders (called Boomers) led by a religious fanatic, opposed by land-hungry range men, and driven from Cheyenne-Arapaho land by sloppy soliders under the command of Lieutenant Winfield Scott Milham, who falls in love with the fanatic's misnamed teen-aged daughter, Silence, and who finds firm purpose only when she is kidnapped. A feature of this novel is the Chaucerian romance of a whiskey peddler and a pioneer female of fading beauty but undiminished drive. Its best feature, however, is Nathan "Running Bear" Frane, a Pawnee graduate of the Indian School at Carlisle, Pennsylvania, who finally responds in the best manner to the Boomer party—he gets out.

First Campaign (1965) came next and is first-rate. It is the first of several Short novels whose setting is at or near Primrose, Junction City, Crater, and other nearby towns probably in Colorado. Short in his Primrose series comes close to creating a Western version of William Faulkner's Yoknapatawpha.[18] The action of *First Campaign* moves to and from Primrose and Junction City, as the hero Cole Halsey and his illegitimate half-brother, Varney Wynn, try to counter the efforts of a decent 1881 gubernatorial candidate's criminal henchmen to unseat Governor Harold Halsey, the father of Cole and Varney. Short introduces a large cast of supporting characters: Burley Hammond, crooked mine owner; sheriffs Sam Morehead and Anse Beckett; Red Macandy, corrupt newspaper editor; Selby and his daughter Louise, of the Primrose House hotel;[19] fat Dave Hardy, owner of the Miners Rest saloon and procurer of villains; and others who also reappear in later Primrose novels. Hammond's daughter Tish has difficulty deciding between heroic and villainous lovers.[20] An innovation here is the inclusion of a juridically cooperative young prostitute, Marty Frost.[21]

Paper Sheriff (also 1965) is also first-rate, with a compelling *donnée:* rancher Reese Branham has been elected part-time sheriff, only to discover the criminality of his wife, Callie, whom he married on the rebound when beautiful assistant district attorney Jen Truro said "no for now" to him. Callie, formerly a Hoad, keeps returning to her tattered but fiercely cohesive clan, which is led by murderous Uncle Orville and can easily muster a dozen rifles. The whittling away of the forces of evil and a surging, credible climax are truly captivating.

With *The Primrose Try* (1966) we return to the locale of *First Campaign*, this time as undercover deputy marshal Sam Kennery tries to solve a murder which disfigures the region still ruled by Governor Halsey and still misreported by Red Macandy. A waitress under the Selbys of the Primrose House is wonderfully spunky little Tenney Payne, whose widowed mother is almost as attractive to Sam. His mission, which is to nail two preposterous villains who make the mistake of hiring him as a killer, takes Sam to an Indian reservation and also up against Seeley Carnes, one of Short's most deadly gunnies.

The action of the excellent *Debt of Honor* (1967) again centers on Primrose, Junction City, and especially Crater, and includes such stalwarts as Burley Hammond, Red Macandy, Dave Hardy, and Louise Selby and her passive father. But the hero's motive is unusual: Reeves Cable seeks revenge on an influential lawyer politician for raping Reeves's foster mother. The presence of the victim's niece from the East results in important East-West contrasts as well as predictable romantic developments. Horrifying violence impedes but cannot stop the hero from successfully completing his mission.

The Guns of Hanging Lake (1968) also dramatizes revenge but this time for the murder of a pleasant, rich British rancher not far from Primrose. A neighbor named Traf Kinnard drops everything to bring a sequence of redoubtable culprits, if not to justice, well then, at least to death. The heroine, Sophie Barrick, is a Zane Grey type, disengaged from the hero because she was domineered by her mother—that is, until Traf persuades Sophie first to help him track the killers and then to hide a key witness.

Donovan's Gun (also 1968) features Jim Donovan of Pitkin, near Primrose and Junction City. He would prefer to remain part-time lawyer and part-time rancher. So he tries, but unsuccessfully, to stay aloof as Will-John Seton, ramrod of Jim's recently deceased neighbor-client Burt Hethridge's spread, sexually consorts with dressmaker Bonnie Leal, who marries young Cole Hethridge, whose sister Sarah then marries Will-John. This sociable arrangement may seem positively Jamesian, but the consequences are not: gunfire-interrupted dance, arson, nester-hired gunslinger Keefe Hart (a funny name when pronounced fast), shootout in a cemetery, and so on to a Jacobean climax which seems a little stagey. Love interest for Jim takes the lovely form of Kate Canady, a Pitkin newswoman.

With *The Deserters* (1969), Short rounds off his impressive 1960s production and in the process returns to a military plot. Lieutenant Peter Brisbin, who is inconsolable because of lost love—as were a few previous Short heroes—welcomes a therapeutic undercover mission. He is to infiltrate the gang of army deserter-murderer Ben Maule, who now owns a dissolute Arizona town close to the Mexican border, and to bring Ben back out at any cost to justice and hanging.

V   *The 1970s*

Three for the Money (1970) has an apt title and a very clever plot situation. A gang kills some guards and steals $160,000 in gold bullion from a railroad train near El Cuervo, Arizona, and the leader hides the heavy loot somewhere in the desert. Three men seek it: Wes Chance, who buried it but has to be careful how he spirits it out again; Bill Crowder, boss of a tough gang which wants to steal it; and hero Cameron "Cam" Holgate, who can save his bankrupt ranch with the reward money. The quest-narrative line is whipsawed by complications: Wes was aided by a beautiful, unprincipled woman named Tina Bowers, whose usefulness to Wes is now finished; and newswoman Amy Cross, though engaged to an incipiently dishonorable sheriff, takes increasing note of Cam's manliness and intelligence. His endurance on the first day of action is beyond belief: in it, the hero enters town, tells the owner of the gold that he will recover it and claim the reward and finger the killers, protects Tina's married sister from Crowder and his men, is slugged unconscious by Wes, recovers and interviews Tina, goes for supper in town, is beaten unconscious by Crowder's men, recovers and shoots one of his captors, and escapes to his hotel room for a snooze. And this is only the beginning.

Man from the Desert (1971), while it has a central male figure as tough and resourceful as the one in *Three for the Money,* is lighter in tone, partly because the hero Hal Hanaway goes about his cleaning up of a messy problem with an almost perpetual chuckle. Ben Kittrick, a banker, mine owner, adulterer, and unexposed criminal in a town near Junction City, has been cheating his sisters, one of whom, Carrie, writes her rancher uncle for help. But the uncle has just died; so Hal, formerly the old man's foreman and now his grateful heir, volunteers his aid. Ben loves but is being looted by Anna Reeves, with the assistance of her off-again lover—supposedly her brother, Dave Reeves. In the sagging middle of the novel, just as Hal is preparing to ride away, Dave bushwhacks Ben and leaves evidence against Hal so incriminating that he must defy the sadistic county sheriff, risk forfeiting a bond, and do detective work which the authorities are too thick-headed to manage. Terrifying scenes follow, some of them set in railroad-construction camps.

With *The Outrider* (1972) Short returns impressively to a familiar scene and to something like the political cauldron we saw bubbling in *First Campaign*. It seems that Governor Sam Kilgore takes bribes from mine owners opposed to costly mine-law reformation. In the fortuitous brief absence of the governor out of state, the crusading lieutenant governor replaces the suddenly deceased attorney general with another crusader; and the two hire the hero, "outrider" Will Christie, to investigate widespread corruption.[22] He only warms up on the libelous, crooked editor of the Granite Forks newspaper; for he then rides into villainy and violence of the first magnitude.

In *The Stalkers* (1973) Short gives us a deputy marshal who is temporarily hampered in his mission of cleaning out a nest of desperadoes because of amnesia: Tim Sefton was shot in the head, stripped of all his possessions, and left for dead in the road.

This before the novel even starts. The book dramatizes Tim's gradual recovery of memory, his assumption of an outlaw identity to infiltrate the gang, and his being helped toward the explosive but then surprising climax by a timorous young woman who works for a local doctor. Uniquely here, the hero spurns the willing young heroine.[23]

Not so in *The Man from Two Rivers* (1974), which pairs two temporary losers. They are Hobart "Hobe" Carew, a rancher driven off his land by an evil county commissioner, and a young girl, Stacey Wheelis, falsely accused of theft. They team up to become winners. The man returns and fights back ingeniously, with the help of a half-breed Indian friend who is often more aggressive than the hero. The girl does her part by opening a boardinghouse, with the help of the Indian's fine native wife. The two main characters converge as a consequence of familiar plot tricks. A switch, however, is that the villain is a villain *manqué;* able to do nothing personally, he is all bluster, bribe, and backdown.

Finally came *Trouble Country* (1976), a posthumously published nightmare of a novel featuring heroic winner against villainous half-brother. Again there is a reluctant sheriff and again arson, as well as a sexy Mexican-American sister-in-law, a psychotic other woman, thieves falling out again, and wife-beating. How Short meets the challenge of having the hero eliminate his half-brother and then propose to his battered widow is less than completely satisfying.

VI *In Sum*

Of Luke Short's fifty-one novels, twenty concern conflict over land, with *Gunman's Chance* and *Ramrod* sharing top honors. In neither is the hero eager to gain land for himself. Nineteen of the books are dominated by the hero's desire for justice, and *Paper Sheriff* and *Debt of Honor* are the best here. Once again, the hero wants justice for others rather than for himself. Seven works concern conflict over identified treasure; here *Hard Money* and *High Vermilion* are the best, and again neither hero wants the object in contention for himself. Three novels are about rivals in business; *The Whip* is the best example. Only two works turn on revenge from the start; *Coroner Creek,* one of Short's supreme successes, illustrates this motive splendidly.

CHAPTER 3

Short's Sense of Place

ACTION is so important in his novels that we may forget that Luke Short always conveys a precise sense of place. With few exceptions, his locus is the West, west of Iowa, Missouri, and Arkansas, north of Old Mexico, east of California, and south of Montana. The states mentioned most frequently in his fiction are Arizona, Montana, New Mexico, and Wyoming. But his plots most often unfold in what would appear to be Colorado.

I Place Names

Short drops names for his places so casually that we need to be reminded of their frequency. For mountains, ranges, peaks, and points, rivers, lakes, creeks, springs, fords, and crossings, canyons, deserts, flats, breaks (and brakes), wells, troughs, and tanks, forts and camps, towns, cities, counties, and states, and related spots, I have counted well over 250 place names—real and fictitious—in Short's novels. It would seem that, like Ernest Hemingway, Short has more faith in place names (and what they stand for) than in either people or their acts. The heroine listens while the hero of *Hard Money* reminisces about Santa Fe, Baja California, and the Canadian Rockies, and then concludes that "always, his talk was of places, not himself" (p. 100). In addition, Short uses vivid names to personalize most of the fictional ranches which pop to the surface of his boiling West.

The most notable instance of his rendering place specific is his creation of the Primrose region. Probably in Colorado, Primrose with its neighboring towns of Junction City, West Haven (also Westhaven), New Hope, Crater, Indian Bend, Pitkin, and Kittrick, watered by its Raft River, and shadowed by the Raft Mountains, should be revered as a major place in Western fiction. The following novels by Short are cast in Primrose or nearby: *First Campaign, The Primrose Try, Debt of Honor, The Guns of*

Hanging Lake, Donovan's Gun, The Deserters, Three for the Money, and *Man from the Desert.* Furthermore, Granite Forks and Congress Junction in *The Outrider* sound and appear like redactions of Primrose and Junction City, while Granite City of *The Stalkers* is at least onomastically close to Primrose as well. In addition, a few other places in other Short novels are reminiscent of Primrose and its neighbors. In creating these Primrose pieces, Short answered a kind of mini-Balzacian, Faulknerian impulse, and did it well.

II   *The West*

The West, in Wallace Stegner's concept of it in his "Wilderness Letter,"[1] is the overriding main fact of Short's sense of place. Hal Hanaway in *Man from the Desert* is tracking a killer into a railroad construction camp, moving ever westward as its steel tracks slink forward, when we read:

> What should he himself do? A train would get him to the end of steel quickest but maybe too soon. Reeves should be given time to reach there and set up his game.
> But Hanaway knew he was purposely deceiving himself. He wanted to ride his dun to the end of the steel, to travel alone in new and silent country, away from towns and people and talk. There had been too much of all three lately. He wouldn't miss any of it—except [the heroine]. . . . (p. 111)[2]

Even in little ways, when caught in civilization's detritus man makes wilderness-tropistic gestures. When Tully Gibbs of *Silver Rock* goes to talk with the old mine owner at the end, we read that, "skirting the rotting boardwalk, he knocked on the door, then turned impatiently to regard the silent night" (p. 149). Just after the sickening climax of *Vengeance Valley*, Owen Daybright makes the same movement away from people to dark, cool, healing nature.

It seems that the West often wants to beat back its would-be conquerors. Facing a "desert floor that held nothing but greasewood, rock mounds, and cactus" and may conceal hostile Apaches nearby, the heroine of *Desert Crossing* comprehensively informs the hero, " 'This is a cruel, cruel country, isn't it, Dave?' " to which he replies, " 'It never lets up on you' " (p. 68).

Sometimes, however, Short adopts a naturalistic attitude toward nature, as when in *High Vermilion* Larkin kills a would-be bushwhacker and lovely nature is indifferent: "When he looked up again, the noon was sunlit, still as a pool, its tranquillity strangely unmarred by this violence" (p. 134). For the most part, only the strongest survive in such a West. Jim Daley, deputy to the hero of *Paper Sheriff,* is so appalled by murder all around him that he brands the villains "a throwback to a jungle he'd hoped he would never have to explore" (p. 135). Jim has little time to philosophize: within a few pages, an amoral creature from this jungle guns him down.

III   *Heights and Snow*

Short expertly handles varieties of scene—the icy Far North, mountains and high country, forests and prairies, water, and deserts. One of his most remarkable scenic effects occurs in *Barren Land Showdown,* when the hero, in an effort to clear himself, agrees to go by airplane with the suspicious authorities to a trapper's camp, to locate the heroine's brother, feared hurt:

Frank watched the country below. Like all men who have traveled the bush and known its hardships, he was filled with an indefinable resentment against the plane. This was too easy; a man lost his perspective. Below them, the black spruce forest stretched out endlessly like clotted bird shot on white paper. The creeks and rivers and lakes were merely part of the background, blank spaces fringed with a gray smear of willows where the bird shot had not rolled. . . . The big white expanse of Horn Lake loomed up ahead of them, barren and cold as death. (p. 97)

Easily the finest handling of snow in all of Short comes in *And the Wind Blows Free,* at the close of which a blizzard hits the hero's herd. Ironically, the storm starts on the day after Christmas, in 1885.[3]

All that morning. . .we watched the winter sky build up behind us, layer on layer of slate-colored clouds that piled up above the low ceiling of the prairie. The air was mild, still as standing water, charged with a breathless expectancy that made our horses uneasy. A little after noon it began to snow gently, the flakes falling as straight as if they were leaded. In mid-afternoon, they took on a slant to the south, and inside of a half hour, the blizzard was on us. It came smoking out of the north, dragging a fathomless darkness with it that rode with snowflakes as small and sharp and hard as glass particles. (p. 111)

The blizzard continues for days and wreaks havoc on the cattle, which stampede but are soon immobilized in a swale by drifts and barbed wire. Most die slowly; and "those still alive had survived only to have their frozen tails break off like icicles, their frozen hooves drop off" (p. 117). The narrator loses his mount, gets lost, and saves himself only by burrowing beneath still-warm, steaming cattle corpses overnight.

Things are usually cleaner at high altitudes in Short's novels. (Here again Short resembles Hemingway.) The desperado-hero of *The Man on the Blue* gallops out of town, climbs past a valley pocket, and makes for the top of a rise; when safe, he enjoys the scenery:

The sun was scarce an hour from setting, and the air was beginning to dissolve into the evening translucence it has in the dry country. The hushed, waiting east stretched before. . .[him], almost to infinity. There off in New Mexico, low mountains lifted their blue *sierras* scarcely higher than the light-green sky of the horizon rim. Closer, the country slanted off into red flats, to fawn-colored dry lands, to purple hills whose every angle was etched in black, and finally to blue of crawling space that had no dimension of perspective. It lay sprawled under the cobalt monotone of the sky, huge, ungrasped, so limitless it exhausted the eye. (p. 103)

This is not to say that murderous action never occurs up toward the peaks in Short. *King Colt, Savage Range, Raiders of the Rimrock, Rimrock,* and *The Guns of Hanging Lake* provide evidence to the contrary. But note the latent symbolism of a slogan over a makeshift canvas bunkhouse in *High Vermilion:*

> *Beds $1.00 a week*
> *No Bugs at This Altitude (p. 17)*

IV   *Forests and the Open Range*

Forests and sparser trees are well sketched in Short. Two especially fine passages occur in *Saddle by Starlight.* Sam Holley's reliable neighbor Will Ferrin loves the morning sounds

of the forests—for example, "the far cry of a jay up in the timber
followed by the distant racheting of a squirrel"—and also the
scenery above: "higher up in the timber and a few minutes climb
was a spot he wanted to see this morning; each night a big buck
came to this spot for his look at the Rafter F below. Ferrin tried
to imagine what insatiable curiosity, what magic of wonderment
pulled the buck, summer and winter, to this spot for a look at a
shining light he could never understand" (pp. 50, 51). Sam
prefers a later hour of the day but is equally in tune with nature:

> The sun had heeled far westward and its slanting light upon the great
> cottonwood by the house seemed to pick out in relief each of its
> thousands of leaves. Somewhere off behind the grain shed Lydia's pet
> goose honked angrily, probably at a cruising ranch dog. In that moment
> of late afternoon stillness this place held a simple goodness for Sam that
> he could never have put into words. He glanced at Julia, wondering if
> she felt it. There was a serenity in her face, too, as she regarded the
> house and beyond it the timbered Elks rising into their cottony
> thunderheads. (pp. 121–22)[4]

The most frequently limned scene in Short is the wide-open
range country. A good example appears early in *Raw Land*.
Returning to the locale of his youth, the hero enjoys a ride early
in the morning of his first full day home: "The country he slowly
rode through during those early hours jogged something in his
memory. He had forgotten what good graze it was, thick, sun-
cured grama grass with the new green thrusting up to crowd out
the old. It was a rolling country, well watered, the hills sloping
down to copses of cottonwoods and willows in the valleys, and
piñon and cedar capping the crests" (p. 16). The finest prairie
scenes appear in *And the Wind Blows Free*. As in several of John
Ford's films Short succeeds in depicting prairie vastnesses by
concentrating on the sky above: "The morning broke windy, with
high clouds shredded over a clean sky. Their shadows raced past
us, scudding across the tilted prairie in ponderous haste" (pp.
41–42).[5] Soon the men smell smoke, come upon a small squad of
prairie arsonists, mow them down ruthlessly, and then fight a
Dantesque fire, which, before long, "was burning the many long
miles to our fence, some fifteen miles distant, eating hourly
deeper into our range, burning forage and trapping cattle, a grim
black desert on the march" (p. 45).

V   *Water*

The most charming lake in Short's fiction is Hanging Lake, in *The Guns of Hanging Lake,* but less for itself than for action near it. "It was a small lake fringed by sparse timber, and on its far shore was a scattering of log buildings. . . . Beyond the buildings and farther up the steep slope were mine tunnels easily spotted by the dumps of waste rock at their entrances" (p. 60). Soon to this natural talus is added human talus—in the form of corpses: this crucial setting, beautiful and harmless in itself, is polluted when greedy people clash nearby.[6]

Action in or very near water is rare in Short. A dramatic flood occurs in *Raw Land,* when a steady drizzle fills an arroyo with "a raging torrent of brown boiling water some thirty yards from bank to bank" (p. 130) and makes the region anything but a suitable battleground between rival villains Milt and Milo. A better depiction of a watery scene opens *The Man from Two Rivers,* as Hobe and Stacey meet unromantically on water: he is paddling a skiff toward a partly submerged sternwheeler to get away from "the sheeting rain bearing down on him" (p. 1), and she is aboard the wreck, defending it from intruders.

The natural sound of smoothly flowing water is restful in Short. Even his oppressed heroes sense it, if but momentarily. In *Coroner Creek,* the creek which provides the title is always singing in the background as it separates the grubby town of Triumph from the genuinely triumphant natural scenes beyond. At one point, "the slow rain and the river's rush hushed his footfalls as he tramped back toward the lumberyard" (p. 131). If the Coroner separates town from ranchers in the country, the Raft River bisects the town of Primrose into the elite and the riffraff. Most of the Primrose novels mention this fact, which is most simply stated in *Debt of Honor:* "Primrose was, Reeves remembered, really two towns, lying in the fold of the last of the foothills before the land heaved up into the timber-clad shoulders of the Raft Range. The brawling Raft River cut the town in two" (p. 22).[7]

VI   *The Desert*

In the Southwest of *Desert Crossing,* the water of the Gulf of California quickly gives way to desert thirst, and when it does so

Short has a chance to describe the scene which he is best at. Over most of the action in *Desert Crossing,* the sun out of a "brassy sky" pours heat which is "blasting," "blasted," "oven-hot," "blazing," "furnace[-like]," "murderously hot," and "seer-ing" (pp. 1, 16, 40, 45, 53, 59, 60, 95, 103, 105, 110). The effect is overpowering and is bearable only because at night a wan but slowly waxing moon presides over scenes somewhat cooler.

Ambush takes places in the same general locale, and its sun is identically "blasting" (p. 56). But here Short takes time to explain that his scout-hero not only endures but enjoys it. "They rested in midmorning and changed flankers and the positions of the detail, and went on again, and Ward sat slack and somnolent in the saddle, feeling the hourly increase in heat. It was dry, savage, merciless, and he liked it. The land, of a sameness that was soporific, was a dun-colored waste of rock and sage clumps and mesquite tangles, and it was never wholly level, so that the twisting road accommodated itself to an endless upthrust of eroded mesa and slope of canyon floor" (pp. 56-57).

To the heroine of *Dead Freight for Piute,* the town of Piute is foreboding because the desert is just outside it and is dominant. "When she mounted the stairs she found she was weary. Too much had happened, and it was all bewildering. Nothing counted here but violence and threats. Everything here was as harsh as the desert that started below the town and stretched out into a terrible fawn infinity" (p. 22).[8] Banning, the town to which his mission takes Pete in *The Deserters,* is dominated by dust. The mines nearby cause dust. It seeps from the mills. It powders the streets and roads. And it especially hovers over the desert to the south, toward Mexico. Pete reconnoiters this likely avenue of escape by the villains. "Once in the saddle and under a cloudless sky, Pete headed south. The country around him seemed bare desert, and the rolling wasteland of rock and sand or of yucca and mesquite and sahvaro baked in the sun" (p. 38).

VII   *Mines and Railroads*

No matter how sublime or awesome a Western region is, Short's materialistic characters come in to mess it up. First they came looking for gold, then silver, coal, and lead (later, uranium); then they drove cattle through, and trails, roads, and railroads followed; and as they pressed in and through, they built ranches, trading posts, way stations, forts, and towns both grubby and pretentious.

Short does not deal with the earliest mining settlements in the Far West before the Civil War. Instead, he usually confines his treatment to the central section of the West, in such novels as *Hard Money, High Vermilion,* and *Silver Rock. Dead Freight for Piute* and *The Outrider* have mining in the background; the main action in the former, however, is hauling ore, while the hero of the latter investigates the illegal or at least unprincipled conduct of rich mine owners. *Barren Land Showdown* concerns a gold mine in the frozen North, but the hero is described as trying for the moment to protect it from others rather than work it. And in *The Deserters* and *Man from the Desert,* and a few other novels, the pervasive grime and the shuddering sounds of mining operations may be constantly in the offing; but the main activity is detective work.

Hard Money depicts mining work in all its technical, dehumanizing aspects, all its color and racket. The opening sentence, which begins the finest first chapter in all of Short, sets the tone for everything which follows: "Booming Tronah [the town] stepped up a pitch at six o'clock evening when the shifts at the mines came off and, like a great lusty and colorful caterpillar, turned over in the cocoon of its own din" (p. 1). Short provides details of mining and pictures of miners at their perilous trade — digging, timbering, handling ore, pumping, dynamiting. Twice he contrasts these sweating have-nots and the fat cats who profiteer from their labor, once by way of a lecture which Phil delivers to the champagne-fancying Sharon, but better when he later takes her to the house of his Swedish shift boss Borg Hulteen and his wife. The account of the Hulteen family, their mellow home, their fragrant kitchen, their songs, and their Old World hospitality is unique in Short.[9]

If Tronah in *Hard Money* is often dusty, the town of Vermilion in *High Vermilion* is dominated by mud. The first miner we meet has "a dark clay-stained suit and muddy boots" (p. 2). When Moffat fights a gunman outside the hotel, the two slip and fall "in the maroon mud," "the red muck" (p. 49) of the street. Meanwhile, Charlie Storrs wonders if his wayward wife, Josephine, can keep her skirts clean in this raw, messy town full of vigorous males. "Charlie noticed that the mud, as it dried, was turning to a red clay. Everything was covered with it—the wheels of the wagons, the legs of the horses, the boots of every man he met. The buildings close enough to the street to be splashed by the wagons were tinted with it. *I'll even bet Josephine picks some of it up on her skirts before she leaves,* he thought sardonically, and then grinned at the thought" (p. 32).[10]

Men not only tear into nature for minerals but also drive passages through nature's lonely stretches for railroad lines. Short rarely deals with this phase of the westward course of empire; but when he does, notably in *Man from the Desert,* the picture is a veritable *Walpurgis Nacht* of the Wild West. To find his runaway quarry, Hanaway rides along the new rail lines for a week, and we read that "the land on both sides of the right of way was scarred and trampled and littered. Hills had been mauled to supply land fill and raw cuts still unrained on slashed through other hills to keep the grade. Everywhere the tent city had been pitched the land had been raped [*sic*] of everything that would burn. It was a vast midden of decaying garbage, cans and bottles, of discarded clothes and boots and broken tools and equipment" (pp. 112–13). Appropriately, it is night when Hanaway gets to the construction camp. The place is lighted by kerosene flares; and, "after a week of solitude, its clamor was an assault on the ears." Soon he smells "the fetid stench of unwashed clothes and sweat and alcohol" (p. 113). We next find tent saloons, tent stores, a big tent with its red lantern outside, and near it the gambling tent which houses Hanaway's target.

VIII *Ranches*

Less damaging to nature are the innumerable ranches scattered through Short's fiction. Many are functional and hence beautiful in his eyes. Thus, the following painterly description, from the early *Marauders' Moon,* is repeated in slightly modified form later:

Before them, at one edge of a deep and wide, grassy valley knifed by a willow-bordered creek, lay the ranch buldings of the Broken Arrow. To Webb, who had traveled through a large part of cattle land, the place spoke to him in his own language. The house itself was a two-story stone affair with a gallery running across the front, and adobe wings branching off on either side [*sic*]. Giant cottonwoods cast their lace umbrellas over it, leaving it deep in shade. Off to the north lay the cluster of sheds and corrals, all solid, all well kept. Between the two lay the long adobe bunk house and cook shack adjoining. All of it had been built for an eye to utility, yet it had achieved a kind of rough beauty that was not all age, and it made Webb look again at Tolleston [the owner]. (p. 32)

By contrast, villains often keep house badly, as Will Christie concludes upon riding onto the turf of some riffraff brothers of Cottonwood Wash, in *The Outrider:*

Presently he broke from between two big dripping piñons, and what he saw made him rein up. Ahead of him, ringed by a scattering of piñon stumps, was a low and small mud-streaked, badly built shack. It had a dirt roof, its corners were uneven, the ridge pole sagged. Immediately around it, and between it and the log shed and corral, there was a litter of rusting bedsprings, a rotting mattress, a wheelless buckboard and a broken grindstone on a carpet of shattered glass from broken bottles. Weeds grew right up to the shack except where they were trampled underfoot. The whole scene bespoke neglect, indifference, and heedless poverty. (p. 145)

The presence of a woman in a ranch house is often a guarantee for Short of its tidiness, but not always. It depends on the woman, and to some extent on her husband or male friend. Thus, the Broken Arrow ranch in *Marauders' Moon* is refined by the touch of Tolleston's nice daughter Martha. In *Raiders of the Rimrock,* another Martha improves her dead father's beautiful spread, near the bottomlands of the Tornado River. The place is not pretty, we read; instead, it is rough and solid, "but its windows had curtains, and there were flowers growing around the door. From the front step many miles of the tree-fringed Tornadoes stretched away in a green ribbon below" (p. 18).[11]

If a woman is spoiled, slovenly, or alcoholic, her home will suffer. Thus, Lee Stobie's opportunistic wife Edith in *Vengeance Valley* does nothing to enhance the rough charm of Acorn, a ranch built on sweat and blood by Lee's father. Nor does Sarah Hethridge in *Donovan's Gun,* either before or after her marrage, beautify the Big House of Triangle H, over which she and her equally worthless brother squabble. Perhaps the least admirable female housekeeper in all of Short is Callie Hoad Branham of *Paper Sheriff.* She throws whiskey, takes a week off for criminal activity after her sheriff husband has been away on business for a week, and dresses in outsized man's clothes. Abbie Miles of *Coroner Creek* is a special case: driven to the bottle by her murderer-husband, Younger Miles, and to a lesser degree by her weak-spined sheriff-father, she is initally indifferent to her home but is redeemed in time and does bake good cookies.

On the other hand, womenless men keep house in accordance with their relative moral worth. Bachelor-hero Jim Donovan of *Donovan's Gun* fully appreciates and dignifies his little ranch, the D Cross. "Jim moved over to the open shelves and took down a bottle of whiskey. This was bachelor's spare kitchen, with a counter on either side of the sink where water was piped in from up canyon. A deal table stood against the wall and three barrel chairs were placed against it. On the other side of the wall was the bedroom" (p. 64).

Ranches in Short which have not only money behind them but, more importantly, family tradition as well are often beautifully appointed inside. For example, Sam of *Bought with a Gun* reports to the owner of Star 22 and is impressed by what he immediately sees: ". . .a large, low-ceilinged room with a floor covered with big Navajo rugs. Its walls held a gun rack, two buckskin ceremonial costumes of some Plains Indians, and a large calendar from a packing house in Omaha. A huge roll-top desk filled one corner, and there were several leather chairs flanking a big fireplace" (p. 39).[12] Sometimes the charm of such traditional Western interiors is lost on thugs. For example, when the villain of *Hardcase* takes over the Big House of Bib M, the spread of the heroine's distraught father, we read simply that "Wallace, whose idea of elegance was a saloon with a tile floor, looked at the rugs, the furniture, the piano from St. Louis, the heavy pink glass lamps, and the curtains. He whistled in awe and then made a wry face. . . then went upstairs to the bedrooms. When. . .[he] came to Carol's room Wallace stepped on the threshold and goggled. There was a fluffy counterpane on the bed; the white curtains were starched stiffly, and there was a lingering scent of lavender in the room" (p. 126).

In the working West, women used to have more to do in the kitchen than in bower or bedroom. Short gives us numerous views of women cooking and baking, serving and scrubbing and sewing. Here are contrasting examples. In *Saddle by Starlight*, Sam gets the heroine, Julia, a kitchen job at Chainlink, the ranch owned by vicious Anse Heth and his admirable wife, Eleanor.

Julia first notes details of the carelessly managed spread—jerry-built sheds, unhooked wheels, scattered harness, dropped tools, loose corral poles, and even boot-mashed flowers—but then enters Eleanor's domain: "The kitchen was a big, pleasant room dominated by a massive black iron range. A table with chairs stood under the window, and there was the good smell of bread baking in the room" (p. 28). The hero of *First Campaign* neglects his girl friend for a while but then heads for her kitchen door to give her some news. "There he had his hand raised to knock when the door swung open and Tish was facing him. She was wearing an apron; her sleeves were rolled up and her hands and forearms were dusted with flour" (p. 144). Tish is right where Cole can find her, in the kitchen where she belongs. But she is so unfeminine in her anger that her movement is revealing: she strips off her apron (symbol of subjugation?), turns the baking over to a servant, and—to talk man-talk with Cole—leads him out of the kitchen.

IX   *Military Forts*

Short did the necessary research to make his sketches of military forts in the late-nineteenth-century American West accurate whether the forts were real or otherwise. For example, in *War on the Cimarron* the vengeful hero rides into Fort Reno but notices less than the reader does the well-depicted parade grounds, stone barracks, sidewalks, sutler's post, wagon yard, feed stable, and blacksmith shop. One town mentioned in this novel as a freighters' terminal is Caldwell, Kansas, 150 miles north. In this town the action of *And the Wind Blows Free* starts. But soon it moves back down to Fort Reno and the adjacent town of Darlington, since the woman the hero loves is married to a captain stationed at the fort. It is also from Fort Reno that the officer-hero of *The Some-Day Country* rides forth both to harass the fanatical Boomers trying to squat in Oklahoma and later to rescue the Boomer leader's abducted daughter, who is finally located up in Alma, Kansas.

In *Ambush*, the New Mexican fort from which the action is mounted is Fort Gamble, the most thoroughly described military fort in all of Short. The second scene of the novel occurs here, as do later ones, including the final one. We visit officers' quarters, enlisted men's barracks and little adobe houses, sundry military

and commercial buildings within the post's walls, corrals and
stables, sutler's post, boardinghouse with veranda, laundry house
and saloon, and parade grounds. Short's narrative does not pause
for ornate descriptions; but we are surely made to sense the heat,
the dust, and the alternate boredom and brutal rush of soldiers'
post life in the Old West.

X *Towns*

When you have seen two Short towns, you have seen them all.
His fictive towns may be divided into shabby, dusty little one-
horse eyesores erupting like pimples on the shoulders and flanks
of Mother Nature—Short calls them "festering towns" once
(*Debt of Honor*, p. 128)—and gaudier, brummagem near-
metropolises such as Primrose trying to pass for diadems
crowning Mother Nature's beauty.

Short's first town is Single Shot: "The Sierra Blancos, towering
a hundred miles of their east-west length in snow-capped
aloofness, must have looked at the town of Single Shot with a
degree of tolerance, since this irregular and shabby cowtown had
been allowed to remain at the mouth of its deep valley for more
than forty years" (*The Feud at Single Shot*, p. 11). The returning
hero looks out a train window at the station on a main street
"fetlock deep in dust, flanked by boardwalks under wooden
awnings and an almost unbroken line of hitchracks," and then at
"false-front stores of weathered clapboard. . .[and] hip-shot
ponies and teams harnessed to buckboards blinking in the light"
(pp. 11, 12).

Malpais Springs, Wagon Mound, Cosmos and Warms, Bend and
Wheeler, Ten Troughs and Seven Troughs, Christian City and
Rincon, San Jon, Morgan Tanks and Peavey, Forks and Hagen,
Piute, Santa Luz, Lobstick, Yellow Jacket, Sun Dust, Boundary,
Signal, Triumph, Rifle, South Pass City, Vermilion and Weed,
Stobie and Gore, Corazon, Relief, Azurite, Ute City and Joash,
Louisburg, Waymarn's Crossing, Harmony, Alma, Bale, Indian
Bend, Pitkin, Banning, El Cuervo, Kittrick, Granite Forks,
Driscoll and Corbett, Two Rivers, and Garrison—this partial list
of towns in Short reads like an unalphabetized index torn from a
dusty Western gazette. With due allowance for some topographi-
cal differences, they coalesce into a stereotype complete with
nearby water, cattle trails and mining roads, corrals and stables,

hotels and tent dorms, saloons, stores, offices, jails, brothels, houses and boardinghouses and makeshift hospitals, privies, and cemeteries.

The killing of one gunman by another in *Ramrod* is staged in a barn by a corral, both authentically sketched as to bawling cattle, lantern, feedbox, hay, stall partitions, walls, and dusty floor.

Crummy hotels in Short are pretty much alike. Serving as an adequate example is the Clearcreek hotel, which the hero checks into early in *The Branded Man.* "The hotel was old and big, its lobby filled with an orderly clutter of miscellaneous chairs that stretched back to the curving desk in a back corner by the stairs" (p. 20). To the picture are soon added key rack, ledger, pen, upstairs rooms off an L in the hall, downstairs dining room, kitchen off it, and often a bar.

One of the most wretched features of mining towns is the canvas-walled flophouse, as foul and degrading as anything in Eastern slums and tenements, which have been more frequently lamented in sociological and naturalistic accounts. Two of the worst tent dorms appear in *High Vermilion* and *First Campaign,* and into both the heroes pursue hired thugs. Outside: "The tent dormitory. . .lay at the edge of a pile of tailings surrounded by scarred and weed-grown land that looked as if it was used as a dump. The dirty gray canvas of the behemoth was billowing in the wind. . ." (*First Campaign,* p. 141). Inside: "Once away from the door and into this airless room, there was a smell that had almost the density of a liquid, and Moffat opened his mouth and breathed through it. It was a raw, choking smell of sweating, unwashed bodies and unwashed blankets and clothes. There was a sound, too, a living animal sound compounded of sighs, snores, faint groans, and the deep exhausted breathing of men; and as Moffat worked his way down the dark aisle between the high tiers, the wretched lot of these men came to him" (*High Vermilion,* p. 18).

Of the dozens of sleazy saloons in Short, most of them with vivid names, this one from *The Outrider* is representative:

He crossed the wide street and went through the swinging doors of the Bullseye Saloon and found himself in a huge, crowded and very noisy room. He stepped away from the doors and halted, waiting for his eyes to adjust to the half-darkness. The bar was a long one and was crowded;

along the wall to the right were benches packed with men; the four big round card tables were not covered with felt, but were bare, and the stools around them, all occupied, were solid sections of railroad ties, too heavy to throw easily. Will noted all this and more too. Heavy wire screening protected the inside of all four street windows and there were no back-bar mirrors and no bottles in sight. In short, this was a miners' saloon, ready for and always expecting trouble. He noted the presence of a cruising houseman, sawed-off pool cue tucked in his belt. (p. 28)

More elegant saloons, often in hotels, feature mahogany bars, mirrors, bottles on display, and booths for private drinking and talk. Tougher saloons are guarded by men on high stools, against the rear wall, with sawed-off shotguns.

The typical store in Short is the hardware store, often with a special section for pigeon-holing mail. Many times the owner of such an establishment doubles as the local undertaker. Sometimes he has a balcony toward the back, and does his books, overseeing, and eavesdropping from that vantage point. His store room in the back, or in the basement, is frequently an arena of nefarious activity.

Offices include lawyers' places of business and sheriffs' work rooms, among similar rooms. The best lawyer's office in Short is that of Jim Donovan of *Donovan's Gun*. It is carpeted but messy with books and papers, has files, a desk with a swivel chair, other chairs, a long table, and windows giving onto the main intersection in town. Often office windows are whitewashed halfway up, presumably to increase privacy. A clichéd treasure of a sheriff's office is the following: "At the sheriff's rear corner office in the big stone courthouse. . . Morehead turned up the lamp on his desk and closed the door. His office. . .could be duplicated in every county seat in the state—the littered desk, the gun rack on the wall, the ancient horsehair sofa for the wounded or the weary, the foul cuspidor for the chewers, and the reward dodgers tacked to the wall" (*The Primrose Try*, p. 21).[13]

One of the most curious offices in all of Short belongs to fat Dave Hardy, who appears in several Primrose novels but whose work room behind his Miner's Rest saloon is best pictured in *Debt of Honor:* "Hardy waddled back. . .into his office. Three of the walls of this room were entirely papered with whiskey posters which made it not only colorful but almost cheerful. Against the

far wall was a roll-top desk, a huge oversized swivel chair facing
it" (p. 28).

Jails are of two sorts in Short, depending on plot requirements.
They may be flimsy, in which case the hero can easily break
out—or in. Or they may be sturdy, in which case the marshal or
sheriff—or hero as surrogate lawman—can make a better·stand
to guard imprisoned ne'er-do-wells. The first cardboard jail in
Short appears in *The Man on the Blue* and is not fireproof. In fact,
the hero escapes from it by setting the place on fire and hiding in
the almost omnipresent roll-top desk, which is then carried out.[14]
The later the novel by Short, the more likely it is to have a more
solid jail. One of the best, in *Donovan's Gun*, has so many thick
steel bars that Will-John, the villain, shoots at but fails to injure
an imprisoned witness because at an angle the cell bars form a
shield.

Brothels do not figure in Short's works until 1965, with the
publication of *First Campaign*, but after that they make up for
lost time and are significant in *Debt of Honor* and *The Stalkers*.

Cole in *First Campaign* traces his half-brother Varney's
whereabouts during a key night. He guesses that the distraught
young fellow might have visited a "sporting house"; so he asks a
friendly saloon keeper to map the red-light district for him and
then goes on a tour. "The first sporting house on his list turned
out not to be a residential house after all, but the second floor of
a saloon." Once inside the parlor, he observes maid, comfortable
chairs, rug, big sofas, and marble-topped table with drinks;
pervading all is the smell of "booze, cheap perfume and cigars."
But Cole has no luck here. So he tries across the street. "This
sporting house was really a house wedged in between two
saloons. Its three steps abutting the plank walk led to a narrow
porch decorated with cut-out gingerbread fretwork. It had once
been painted white but now it was a dingy gray" (pp. 130, 132).
Its parlor resembles the first one but also has fancy sideboard,
upright piano, and red-velvet curtain.

The brothel in *Debt of Honor* is more ornate, perhaps because
the prostitute needed as witness in this novel—she is colorfully
named Pony—plays a more significant role in the plot. She is a
dancehall and percentage girl at the Cameo, a two-story saloon
whose second floor has "cribs" for assignations. Short colorfully
depicts the area near Pony's little upstairs billet—"red wallpaper
with gold fleur-de-lis printed on it" (p. 120), parlor with black

leather sofas, corridor beyond curtain of red velvet, and so on.

It might be expected that Short's fiction would be peppered with cemetery scenes, but not so. The only big one occurs in *Donovan's Gun*, when we read that a victim from each side in the violent feud between Triangle H and the nesters is to be buried, at 10:30 A.M. and 11:00 A.M., respectively. The *Hamlet*-like comic relief provided by the lugubrious conversation between undertaker and sexton occurs against a backdrop of cemetery gates, cottonwoods, headstones, raw-earth mounds, ornamental fences, decorative flowers, board-supported plain pine coffins, funeral coach, tool shed, hitch post, tree-lined road, cemetery lanes, and the like. Since the first group of so-called mourners arrives late and the second early, gunplay follows and soon more graves are needed. The scene is grotesque in the extreme.

The festering quality of the small town is present in Short's larger, grander towns as well; but it is usually covered by an overlay of pseudocivilization. Thus, Primrose is not materially different from the bigger, more pretentious Junction City, in the several Primrose novels. Primrose, with ranches and mines in its environs, has its divisive river too, and hotels, stores and offices, sporting houses, railroad station, and saloons of varying degrees of respectability and violence. Junction City has all of this plus state government buildings and newspaper offices. The elements which make Junction City more pretentious than Primrose may also make it more Eastern and hence less necessary for our purposes here.

XI *Indian Locales*

Never do we find the locale of Indians described by Short in romantic terms, in terms expected and conventional according to patterns established by earlier Western fiction writers. Instead, Short usually shows his Indians sporting on beef-issue day, enduring a degraded reservation life, or suffering humiliation in other ways. "Below the huge corral filled with bawling beef the mass of Indians was gathered. They made a wild and colorful picture, the men on horses and clotted in small groups, the women and children afoot, many of them seated on skins. Whether Arapaho or Cheyenne, they favored the gaudiest of blankets and clothes and seemed to mix without regard to tribe. Already, a hundred small fires had been built and the children

and women were scouring the timber on the river bank for fuel"
(*And the Wind Blows Free*, p. 21).

The best of a small number of reservation scenes is the one in
The Primrose Try, in which the undercover hero takes a train
from Primrose north to Junction City and on to Boundary, then a
stagecoach toward the reservation, near Crater. He shops at a
smelly trading post, which offers for sale untanned hides, coal oil,
dress goods, denim pants, socks, blue blankets, lanterns, nails,
dried fruit, jerky, and whiskey. Once on the reservation, he sees
tepees, children at play, mounted Indians on the road, the agency
buildings, corrals, and stock pens under cottonwoods, and all the
predictable accoutrements.

An act of physical and symbolic humiliation of an Indian
transpires early in *And the Wind Blows Free*, out on the lone
prairie. First the setting: "Here was nothing, only space and grass
and low hills belonging to the Indians who only ten years before
had risen to massacre the white settlers to the north, and who
were again threatening our people. As a red winter sun set that
evening, touching the snow patches with pink before cold
darkness rolled in from the east, I knew the full meaning of being
a stranger in a strange land" (p. 9). Two horsemen ride up,
Indians demanding money from the white party, of which the
young narrator is a greenhorn member. For answer, the
stagecoach driver gets down, walks over to one of the Indians,
and without a single word breaks his nose with "a tearing,
slippery" blow of his fist (p. 10). The other Indian rides away,
and the white men have a laugh. Strangers in a strange land. . . .

CHAPTER 4

Short's Characters

S HORT'S characters may be divided into his heroes and their friends (if any), lawmen, villains, and heroines and other women. Short also employs a few Indians, including half-breeds, although they rarely figure in protracted action. His few fictional children are usually little boys who run errands.[1] His image of Western society is thus harsh and adult, a group largely composed of "lawless sheriffs and honest desperadoes," to use Daniel J. Boorstin's revealing phrase.[2]

I *Heroes*

The first thing we learn about a typical Short hero is his physical appearance. Nearly all of these men are big and strong, muscular but lean, graceful, and capable of great endurance. The hero of *King Colt* is depicted thus: "Of the four men seated at a rear table in the Kiowa Head, Johnny Hendry was easily the tallest. . . . His walk [when he moves to the street for a fight] was lithe, effortless, and there was a tolerant good humor about his pleasantly lean face that placed him apart from the rest of the men. . . ." (p. 9). Jim Wade of *Savage Range* is similar, although a long ride in the rain has soured him for the moment. "Erect, he was a tall man, his slicker showing only his overwide flat shoulders and hiding the lean hips and the long, hard legs. . . . The match he struck showed his face in bright and momentary relief, and it was an amused face, one primed for trouble and laughter and daunted by long, hard rides" (p. 9). Our first glimpse of the hero of *War on the Cimarron* is hardly different: ". . .Frank rode in among them. Seen in this dusk, he was unmistakably Texan, tall and bleach eyed and narrow hipped. Without dismounting he leaned wearily on his saddle horn, thumb-prodded his Stetson back off his forehead and scrubbed a

lean, browned and beard-stubbled jaw with the flat of his hand"
(p. 2).

Only a few of Short's heroes are smaller than average, but they
are still not to be trifled with, as an indefinable something in
their appearance ought to suggest to would-be goaders. Here is
the first image of Poco St. Vrain, hero of *Bold Rider:* "He was
young, under middle height, and now he stretched and yawned
with an indolent economy of movement that was as clean and
alert and contained as a cat's" (p. 6). So with Sam Teacher, hero
of *Bought with a Gun:* "Erect, without his shirt, he was
undersize. His chest and shoulders were solid and beautifully
knit without being heavy. His face. . .was tough, arrogant
beneath his tow-colored hair" (p. 9).[3]

What of their heroic facial features? Often, these man have
dark coloration. Poco's "eyes. . .[were] dark to blackness"
(*Bold Rider,* p. 6). Giff Ballew's "blue eyes were tranquil under
thick jutting black brows" (*First Claim,* p. 2). Lee McPhail has
"eyes. . .so black they seemed pupilless" (*Last Hunt,* p. 6). If the
hero's eyes are gray, they sometimes inspire poetic description,
as when Short tells us that Shamrock Ireland's "eyes were rain-
gray, and had the opacity of slate, the surface lights of agate"
(*The Man on the Blue,* p. 6). Occasionally these men are green-
eyed, have black hair sometimes shot with gray, and are once in a
while red-headed. An interesting facial feature of a few is
broken, badly set noses—badges of former fights. At least the
following heroes are so decorated: Tully Gibbs (*Silver Rock*),
Keefe Calhoun (*Summer of the Smoke*), Reeves Cable (*Debt of
Honor*), and Will Christie (*The Outrider*). In addition, many of
Short's heroes are endowed not only with rock-firm jaws, which
jut and sometimes even display corded tendons and ligaments,
but also with shoulder and back muscles frequently said to
resemble ropes.

An old warhorse of a rich miner's wife in *Hard Money* tellingly
praises newcomer hero Phil Seay to Sharon Bonal, who seems
reluctant to recognize his charms: " 'Young woman, hard-bellied
men like that are so scarce in this camp that I don't intend to
stand on ceremony.' " She boldly invites him to her party. Later,
Sharon's father silently commends Phil in identical terms, and
more: "The thought of Seay warmed something inside Bonal and
gave him a kind of impersonal strength. There was *his* kind of
man, with a hard belly and hard fists and a brain inside his hard

skull, a man who would rather fight than eat, and who had the strength to be gentle" (pp. 41, 76).

Most established men lack the insight and generosity to praise Short's tough heroes. Bruce McFee, the heroine's father in *Hardcase,* for example, dislikes little Dave Coyle and therefore, although he needs him, tells him off. " 'Coyle, I don't like you. . . . But you're shrewd. I'll give you credit for that. You've got gall—enough for a hundred men. And you've got a queer kind of reckless guts that I don't rightly under-stand. . . . [R]ight now I need you.' " To which Dave brashly replies: " 'McFee, . . . I don't like you either. You're a hardheaded Scotchman without anything but money and temper. . . . You're bull-headed and you're tough. But you're the wrong kind of tough, McFee. You're tough on the little people—the people that can't help themselves. . . . I'll throw in with you and help you because your girl is human, and she's in trouble. . .' " (pp. 57–58).[4]

Such comments move us into a consideration of the virtues and vices of Short's heroes. Of the seven cardinal virtues, these fiery men exemplify only justice, courage, temperance, and hope, and fail to worry much about prudence, faith, and real charity. To prove that they are a strange mixture of virtue and vice, Short endows some of his heroes with inordinate pride and monumen-tal anger, although of the remaining seven deadly sins—lust, envy, avarice, gluttony, and sloth—they are regularly free.

An even-handed, level-headed desire for impersonal justice motivates many of Short's heroes. For example, Tim Enever (*Raiders of the Rimrock*) rides into a strange region to bring peace to an area torn by strife between cattlemen and sheepherders. Ward Kinsman (*Ambush*), although he admires the Apache way of life, agrees to recapture a renegade leader of breakaway Apaches and rescue their white female captive. And Sam Kennery (*The Primrose Try*) is brought into the Primrose region to smoke out an unknown murderer. Often the yearning for justice is more personal, as when Reeves Cable (*Debt of Honor*) readily answers his foster mother's plea to ruin her rapist, when Traf Kinnard (*The Guns of Hanging Lake*) drops every-thing to find a likable neighbor's vicious stabber, and when Hal Hanaway (*Man from the Desert*) breaks up family injustice as a favor to a dead friend.

Sometimes Short's heroes mete out justice with a vengeance,

taking the prerogative from the Lord, and exacting the
Churchillian two eyes for an eye and for every tooth a jawbone.
To be sure, revenge is a kind of folk justice; but often Short's
heroes go awfully far. And in the process, concern for the truth
never deters them. To achieve a good end, they connive, disguise
themselves, and lie with great dash. Reeves Cable (*Debt of
Honor*) puts it best when he carefully explains to the Eastern
heroine: " 'Beth, we're dealing with a whore and a man who took
a bribe. . . . . They expect dishonesty from other people.' He
paused, then added dryly, 'Let's not disappoint them' " (p. 68).[5]
On the other hand, however, when Sheriff Ben Judd (*Three for
the Money*) lets the heroine lie to enhance his dwindling
reputation, she thinks less of him afterwards, even though the lie
was her idea.

In achieving their missions, Short's heroes display epical
courage, against odds which in ordinary earthly combat or mere
literary tragedy would result in posthumous glory. But in Short
the heroes always win. Sometimes they are so brave and
ingenious that they precisely qualify as figures in the high
mimetic mode, in Northrop Frye's sense—that is, they "are
above our own level of power and authority, though within the
order of nature and subject to social criticism."[6] Thus, Mark
Flood (*The Branded Man*) and Tip Woodring (*Bounty Guns*),
among others, are so anxious to work their purpose that they
courageously walk into the middle of feuds, succeed, and survive
unscathed. The courage of Cole Armin (*Dead Freight for Piute*)
is systematically and mysteriously tested. Who pushed Ted
Wallace down the stairs and broke his leg? Who sawed the brake
lever of the ore wagon? Who burned down Monarch's barn and
shop? And who blew up the China Boy mine?[7]

One way of displaying courage is to endure wounds with
indifference. In each of Short's most representative novels, the
hero is badly wounded. Jim Garry of *Gunman's Chance*—"When
it hit, Jim felt an agonizing pain under his ribs as a knife tore into
his chest, seared along a rib and then buried itself in his flesh" (p.
168). Dave Nash of *Ramrod*—"He saw the man's rifle come to
his shoulder, saw the flash, and then something hit his body with
stunning force and knocked him sprawling to the ground." He
disposes of his assailant; then "sat up now, feeling his chest and
belly warm with a wet stickiness,. . .put his hand inside his
shirt. . .and. . .felt his shoulder, and this time it was as sore to

his touch as the end of an exposed nerve. The pain of it shocked him into an awareness that his blood was steadily soaking his clothes. . ." (p. 124). Chris Danning of *Coroner Creek*— ". . .Ernie stamped three. . .times, the sharp high heel of his boot thudding with a thick muffled sound on Chris' hand and skidding off each time, ripping a great furrow in the skin" (p. 58). And tough, graying Will Gannon of *The Whip*—

And then the big sound came and a tearing agony slammed at his back and side, knocking him flat on his face into the dirt of the corral. . . .

In those terrible seconds while he struggled to replace the air driven from his lungs, he was certain he was going to die. With a massive effort that engulfed him in pain, he rolled over, shot toward the corner of the barn, and then was wretchedly aware that men and horses were running, whether at him or away from him he did not know, for he was drowning in an ocean of pain. (pp. 68, 69)

Jim, Dave, Chris, and Will all fight back, and survive. Other Short heroes are also beaten, stabbed, and shot. They also fight back to victory.

Short's heroes are temperate in all regards save in generously dispensing mayhem. They may wolf down their food when they are hungry, but they eat only to sustain their drive for gory justice. They toss off much whiskey but never to elevation—as Ben Franklin would say. They enjoy cigarettes, cigars, and pipes, especially in the éarlier books; but only villains chew.

It almost never occurs to a Short hero, once he is on the rampage toward the target of his animosity, to figure on anything but final victory. Thus, they usually typify resplendent hope. What they hope for might not please traditional moralizers; but their expectation that things will work out with a kind of fatal rightness is an illustration of traditional, if temporarily eclipsed, American optimism. For example, Short punctuates the entire length of *Coroner Creek* with italicized, Faulknerian inner thoughts by the hero to the effect that he will do as he wishes. "*If I work for him* [his enemy], *I can pick the time and the place to kill him. And tell him why.*" "*Now it'll happen.*" "*His luck is that he'll die.*" "*I can get on with it now.*" "*I can kill him now.*" And "*I could crowd him every minute until I broke him*" (pp. 15, 21, 50, 103, 104, 111). Here Chris is almost his own divinity, in whom he has absolute trust. In *Three for the Money,* Cam

Holgate cockily says to the man who has lost the gold shipment and has posted a reward for its return, " 'Take a good look at me. . .I'm the man you'll be paying' " (p. 4). Through the ensuing struggle Cam never abandons hope.

II *Friends*

In the ranks of the friends of Short's heroes, we find young idolizers, fellow gentlemen in the rough, hardcases—even criminals—former enemies, and old-timers. Young Joel Hardy, the narrator of *And the Wind Blows Free*, looks up to the flawed hero Jim Wade even though the man is in love with a married woman; Joel occasionally acts as Jim's conscience. Link Thomas, the villainess's calf-eyed, teen-aged ranch hand in *Ramrod*, gradually turns to the hero as to a surrogate big brother. And Will Gannon of *The Whip* admirably takes orphaned Bert Dickert, aged about sixteen, under his wing and offers him a bookkeeping job. One of the finest touches in the entire range of Short's fiction occurs later, when, wounded and thought dead, Will while in hiding orders a trusted stagecoach driver thus: " 'Have Dickert report. . . . Tell Dickert I'm alive, but no one else. . . . No one' " (p. 88). Will can trust no one so fully as he can the kid Bert.

Friends as stalwart as their heroes are common, starting with Short's first novel, *The Feud at Single Shot*, in which Dave Turner is shown to rely on redhead Rosy Rand and gambler Martin Quinn. Sadly, some of Short's heroes place faith in associates who are false, as happens, for example, when Will Danning (*Raw Land*) aims at a low profile in order to hide a friend who turns out to be guilty both of past crime and of present disloyalty. Frank Nearing (*Barren Land Showdown*) is betrayed more appallingly by a "friend." In a few novels, the daring example of the hero inspires conscience-stricken gun hands on the wrong side of the fence to reform. So it is with Scoville (*Savage Range*) and Pete Framm (*Sunset Graze*). Short rewards both penitents with brides at the end.

Old-timers comprise an interesting group of friends of heroes, again starting with the first novel. In *The Feud at Single Shot*, crotchety Laredo Jackson appears late, in Chapter 11: "The stranger was a small man, mounted on a big roan gelding that made him look like a wizened monkey-faced little jockey. He had great, drooping sandy mustaches that were generously shot with gray." His first words? " 'Howdy' " (pp. 89, 90). He is feisty, resourceful, and loyal. Old Ives the wolfer similarly enters the action of *Sunset Graze:* "He was an old man, small, wiry, and he moved down the rutted street as noiseless as smoke, his moccasins barely whispering as he moved. In front of the Olympus he paused among the horses tied there, stroking them absently, looking past the lower half of the windows, which were painted an opaque and peeling white, into the saloon" (p. 22). He too is resourceful: his Indian ways—symbolized by his gliding, moccasin-clad tread—save the hero's life. So too with the best old-timer in all of Short, old Asa Caskie, much-sought witness to a murder (*The Guns of Hanging Lake*): "He was a tall, stooped old man dressed in a filthy buckskin jacket and pants that held buckskin patches and he wore Indian moccasins whose tips curled up at the toes. His thick white hair needed cutting and his month's beard was the same color as his hair, but it was patchy, giving him the appearance of a mangy dog. The skin of his upper face and forehead was weather-burned and he stank of whiskey and a decade of campfire smoke" (p. 2).

The doom of some of the heroes' friends is signaled early in a few of Short's novels. For example, Bill Schell (*Ramrod*) and Hutch Forney (*The Whip*). Our first information about Schell comes from Dave Nash's hard-luck girl friend, who says, " 'You know Bill. He'll hang around town for a week drinking and playing poker and camping in my lap with some friend, and all of a sudden he's gone' " (p. 7). Later, after he has killed an opponent in a manner violating the Western code, alert readers know that Bill must die and only hope that the manner of his taking off will aid Dave—and it does. As for Hutch, his fate is almost identical: this friend of Will Gannon's is married to an Indian, neglects their children, is a womanizer, and—worst of all—is derelict in his duties as Will's employee. Obviously his days are numbered, but his murder provides the hero with his final motivation.

The canniest friend of any Short hero is Jim Byers, Hobe Carew's daring half-breed Indian partner (*The Man from Two Rivers*). Oddly, it is Jim, not Hobe, who brings about the noisy climax and saves the day. The most generous friend of any hero is Pearly Gates (*Bought with a Gun*), who quits his job as foreman at the Star 22 ranch, uses his considerable savings to buy a saddle shop next to the Santa Luz jail, and tunnels from his shop into that establishment to free the hero Sam Teacher—all because Pearly admires Sam's snappy method of handling the ranch owner's son and thus believes in Sam's innocence.

III *Lawmen*

More often than not the hero of a given novel is indifferent to the law if not positively antagonistic, unless of course he is a lawman himself, in the open or undercover, or a military upholder of the law.

If I had to list the ten best lawmen in all of Short, they would be Corporal Millis (*Barren Land Showdown*), Ernie See (*Hardcase*), Jim Crew (*Ramrod*), Lieutenant John Haven (*Station West*), Lieutenant John Overman (*Desert Crossing*), Reese Branham (*Paper Sheriff*), Sam Kennery (*The Primrose Try*), Barnard (*Man from the Desert*), Will Christie (*The Outrider*), and Tim Sefton (*The Stalkers*). What these men have in common, in addition to courage, is a willingness to forget the letter of the law to see that higher justice prevails. Millis reserves judgment, gives the suspect hero extra time, tampers with evidence, and is forgiving. See, a deputy under a foolish sheriff, is long-suffering, illegally aids the fugitive hero, risks his job, and wins. Crew coldly goes about his job, knowing the odds, facing death at the hands of laughing evil, and dying with a wintry purity on his features. Haven is a man for all seasons. Overman is the best of a few Short soldiers in uniform who carry out orders with loyalty, ingenuity, and panache. Branham is the first hero in Short who is an admirable nonmilitary lawman. Kennery, an undercover deputy marshal like Sefton later, is motivated to combat crime because his fiancée was killed in some irresponsible cowboys' crossfire earlier. Barnard has survived too long to call it quits and find a rocking chair; he uses pseudosenility like a concealed weapon. Christie is the most stoical of Short's quasi-legal heroes, although for lumps some of Short's other extralegal male figures have him beaten.

Subsidiary lawmen who support heroic action in Short are numerous enough but not outstanding very often. For example, Sheriff Buck Hannon (*Fiddlefoot*) is personable but by himself does little until the hero precipitates climactic action, at which time the sheriff becomes a plot-tidying nemesis. Con Alvis

(*Vengeance Valley*) epitomizes the good law-enforcement agent. Early in the story he breaks up a would-be saloon brawl between hero and villain. After he orders the hero to desist and the hero truculently asks, " 'Who'll stop me?' " we read "Con Alvis had the point of his skinny shoulder against the frame of the door between parlor and bar. An oversize pistol dangled from his bony hand, and he regarded Owen with an old man's disillusioned, mournful eyes that held no indecision at all. 'I will,' he said gently" (p. 13). Later Con hustles the villainous Fasken brothers out of town; but they sneak back, and justice must be dispensed from a six-gun barrel.

Short heroes often rely on friendly and fairly capable lawmen. A good example is Sheriff Frank Cosby (*Last Hunt*), who professionally helps Lee McPhail find a killer even though Frank is Lee's unsuccessful rival for the heroine's hand—and sexual defeat rankles.[8] A better example of a good, plodding tin-star man is Anse Beckett, who plays a minor supporting role as sheriff of Primrose County in *First Campaign* and is essential to the success of the hero of *Debt of Honor*. Without asking for premature explanations, Anse simply does what Reeves Cable tells him—runs errands, reports information to him, escorts witnesses to his hotel room, puts a person in protective custody when told to, obtains a search warrant to locate he knows not what, and so on. But toward the end Reeves is in a quandary, because, as he explains to Pony, " 'I can't arrest him [the villain] and I can't get the killer. Beckett can do both. . . . You see, Pony, it all comes back to having the law act on this because we can't' " (p. 124). These are words published in law-and-order 1967. An earlier Short hero would not be caught shot saying such words.

The first sheriff Short ever created is Hank Lowe of *The Feud at Single Shot*. He is typical of a couple of dozen paunchy, sluggish, graying lawmen who are predictably unequal to any task. He is a caricature. "Dave turned. Confronting him was a fat, shapeless man, looking like nothing so much as two hundred-odd pounds of soiled clothing topped by a greasy Stetson. He wore ragged, saber mustaches below a thick-nostriled nose and his eyes were colorless, unblinking, red-rimmed. Where his chest sloped to his belly, a star reposed, the only neat thing about him except the twin butts of Colts that sagged just above his knees" (p. 12).

Sometimes a sheriff of only indifferent abilities comes to the aid of the hero in a ghastly way. Sam Honeywell, marshal of Clearcreek (*The Branded Man*), in hopeless admiration for the heroine and guarding her departure from town after her brother's funeral, calmly sights from ambush with a rifle on the belly of a man following her for no reason and blasts him out of the saddle. "He didn't bother to go down and look at the man. He knew he was dead. He knew, too, who the man was, and he found a kind of comfortable and stern relish in the thought that he had been wanting to do just this thing to Breckenridge for a long time" (p. 136).

We must conclude that if a good-enough sheriff does not successfully hinder the hero in a Short novel, he is forgivable, whereas if a so-so sheriff aids the hero regardless of legal niceties, he is positively commendable. Naturally, if lawmen oppose the hero—and several try—they are no good and are in for trouble. The first such lawless sheriff in Short is deceptive Andy Lobell (*The Man on the Blue*), whom Shamrock saves early in the novel from the heroine's justifiable wrath only to learn the hard way later that soft-talking Andy's inclination for white peppermint drops deodorizes total villainy. Similarly, deputy Johnny Hendry (*King Colt*) learns that his boss Baily Blue is corrupt. Sheriff Ed Linton (*Dead Freight for Piute*) is on the take and willing to kill to preserve his domain. Significantly, after the start of World War II, Short depicts only one major lawman as thoroughly corrupt. He is Sheriff Ben Clay, town of Corbett, who in *The Stalkers* shakes down June Constable, leader of the gang operating near Driscoll. Oddly, although the hero penetrates June's territory and kills the scoundrel, Sheriff Clay vanishes over the hill and back to his sanctuary—a curiously modern conclusion to this 1973 novel, which is nonformulaic in other ways as well.[9]

IV *Villains*

From corrupt marshals, sheriffs, deputies, county commissioners, and governors, it is only one step down to Short's out-and-out villains, of whom every one of his novels has at least one. These villains are motivated with almost monotonous regularity by avarice. In addition, they are often guilty of pride, anger, and gluttony. Only rarely are they lustful, and then but incidentally;

never are they slothful but instead often display terrifying energy. Several of the novels have a main villain each, with an assortment of repulsive henchmen at his beck and call, devoted to him with a loyalty almost admirable. Rarely do such cronies think of deserting. Often Short peels them away from the primary villain in skillfully managed action charged with drama. The fate of primary evil is almost always death.

One of the most unappetizing villains in all of Short's works is R. B. Jarboe (*High Vermilion*), the greedy mine owner who tries to force out competition by all means possible. Here is our first picture of him:

Jarboe was a sagging, dirty man whose ageless slack face was always framed with white beard stubble. One loose jowl was paunched comfortably by a cud of tobacco; a thin line of stained spittle trickled from either corner of his mouth, and from his pendulous underlip, and Moffat, seeing this, knew why the kids of the town followed his buggy yelling, "Hello, one-eleven!" His pale eyes, however, held no suggestion of age or frailty; they were as blunt as shiny brass, and only a little darker in color. He was a big mine owner, mine broker, streetcorner banker, and a trader who would and could turn a profit on any machinery that moved or shack that stood up or man that worked. (p. 21)[10]

Such a man needs a gunslinger to back him up, and Bill Taff fulfills that function.

Another soft-spoken villain, also proud of his brains and rightly so, is Servel Janeece (*Hard Money*), who like Jarboe enriches himself on the sweat and blood of common miners. Through a lesser villain's eyes we first observe him: "Servel Janeece, a frail ghost, sat on the. . .[desk] corner. . . . He wondered idly if Janeece was consumptive. . . . The pallor of the man's face was almost luminous, heightened by dead-black clothes and a loosely knotted black tie. Janeece was a small man, and he had a small tired voice, but his was not the small man's way, for it was the opposite of aggressive. He was utterly reasonable, quietly and apologetically logical and ruthless as death. His dark eyes always held a sardonic reserve which he never voiced" (p. 43). Short unfortunately fails to develop this spidery financier, who is built—like John D. Rockefeller—to accumulate and survive.

Martinetlike, almost military villains are not common in Short but do exist. Major Fitz of the Bar 33 and seven other ranches

(*King Colt*) best represents this kind of character. "Major Fitz
was much smaller than the two punchers who joined him at the
bunkhouse. . . . Cavalry regulations would have frowned on his
dress—half-boots with a three-inch stockinged gap to his tight
army trousers; a hunting-coat of duck over a cotton singlet; and
an oversize Stetson—but they would have commended his
straight carriage, his bowed legs, his sharp, wind-reddened face,
and his air of authority. His voice and his restlessness combined
to give him the effect of a terrier, but his heart was that of a St.
Bernard. . ." (pp. 20, 21).[11]

Short's three deadliest all-purpose villains are without question Tate Riling (*Gunman's Chance*), Frank Ivey (*Ramrod*), and
Will-John Seton (*Donovan's Gun*). They are all big, canny,
ruthless, opportunistic, heavily handsome, and fast. Ivey is
probably Short's most accomplished bad man. We first meet him
thus: ". . .he turned his head, tilting it up a little to see Dave, and
a brief dim light from the lobby touched it. It was a cold square
face and might have been blocked out of granite, and the
arrogance of its full jowls and broad, thin-lipped mouth was
regal. The gesture of looking at Dave held a magnificent
contempt. . . . The man, Dave thought narrowly, did not know
fear" (pp. 18-19). Later, we learn about this man's primitive
philosophy concerning women: ". . .he knew no man alive was as
stubborn as he was—or woman either for that matter. He'd have
Connie some day, if only through wearing down her resistance.
Besides, he admired her spirit. He didn't want a meek, demure
wife; he wanted a woman with fire and a mind of her own, and
Connie had both. It never occurred to him that she might, in the
end, refuse to marry him. He was the best man he knew, and
that's what any woman wanted" (p. 60). But he reckons without
the better-controlled energy of Dave Nash, the hero. At the
beginning of the inevitable shootout, Dave, rested and poised
(though recently wounded), steps into the street, to make
himself visible. Frank starts to walk toward him; but ". . .then, as
if some overpowering impatience was driving him toward this
moment, he started to run toward Dave, who stopped." Frank
fires hastily, is shot, sits, moves his gun like a club and fires again,
is shot again as he aims his third shot; then he falls on his back,
gets to his knees, stands again, turns: "He was bleeding at the
mouth now, and his black eyes were terrible with death. . ." (p.
214).

Lesser villains abound in Short. The one with the neatest scheme is Rig Holman (*Bounty Guns*), a saloon keeper who on the side killed a man who had made a secret gold strike; Rig then hires the hero to seek the victim's killer in the hope that the man will unwittingly stir up trouble between local feuders, leaving him free to step in and jump the gold claim somehow. Lute Westock (*Barren Land Showdown*, 1940, 1951) is one of the most evil of villains: he is a saboteur during World War II, then in the revision during the Korean War; he is also a poisoner and a woman killer on the run. Senator Maitland (*Hardcase*), Justin Rankin (*Debt of Honor*), and Governor Sam Kilgore (*The Outrider*), are all Establishment figures whose hypocrisy and double-dealing know no bounds. Younger Miles (*Coroner Creek*), Brick Noonan (*Desert Crossing*), and Ben Maule (*The Deserters*) all have criminal pasts, pose as something they are not, and must come to grief in the gory process of Western exposure. They are living disproof that the West is undeviatingly the land of the safe second chance.

The most cunning and depraved gunmen in Short are Espey Cardowan (*Bold Rider*), Richie Cleff (*The Whip*), Seeley Carnes (*The Primrose Try*), and Jud Phillips (*The Stalkers*). All are proud of their professional reputations, only one is sexually villainous (Jud is evidently perverted), and each comes to death in a way appropriate to his type of evil—as do most of Short's villains. Here is the worst gunman, in quick strokes: "Richie Cleff had derisive dark eyes that burned like a banked fire, promising total wildness when anger came. His lean, unshaven face held a dormant viciousness and now he. . .jeer [ed]. . . ."[12] Later, just before his death, we read, "There was an animal ferocity in Cleff's thin face, a will to kill in his eyes that went beyond any declaration in words. . . . If Cleff was afraid there was nothing in his face to show it, and in that moment Will knew that the man feared nothing. The thought of it was suddenly intolerable to him. Here was a butcher cornered at last, and his only answer to the charges against him was to spit contemptuously." So Will prepares to lynch him; then we read, "For the first time Will saw something like fear mingled with the wild hatred in Cleff's eyes" (pp. 9, 99, 100, 101).

The most demented killers in Short are Albie Meacham and Otey Bliss (*Saddle by Starlight*), a pair of so-called homesteaders whom villainous Hugh Ganley has hired and now judges thus:

". . .neither. . .had ever been a boy, Ganley thought; they had
been old and wise [not so] and vicious at birth. They were the
happyhearted, ageless, hog-ignorant products of a frontier,
vaguely southern, that Ganley had never seen and could only
guess at—throwbacks to an earlier and earthier roughness. He
had written a Texas friend to send two men up and this was the
pair he drew" (pp. 36–37).[13] An emphasized characteristic of the
pair is their smell. Their employer once seeks them out in their
rooming house: "When Ganley entered its odorous corridor that
morning he could smell unwashed clothes, the lingering stench of
whiskey, of old leather and of long unaired rooms" (p. 101).
Their most sadistic act is to beat a defenseless man to death with
bricks in a dark alley: "Once in their own private world of
darkness Otey and Meacham played their drunken game. . . .
The game went on until they were both exhausted. It was played
without any anger, without any thought and without any
recollection of why it had started" (p. 49).

A minor sort of villain in Short is the dishonest Indian agent.
He is typically fat, slovenly, and pusillanimous. Among the
several who dirty the scene in the few Short novels in which
reservations and trading posts appear is Mitchell Baines (*Trouble
Country*), "a heavyset man with a ponderous belly and a black
beard"; he is soon said to have a "grossly fat figure [and]. . . a
gray-shot full black beard that matched in coloration his thick
hair. Incongruously, he wore a townsman's dark business suit"
(pp. 115, 116). Bureaucratic sinners in Short are regularly
exposed but often are not further punished.

V Women

The women in Short's novels are of three types. They are
demure, hardworking, patient, and appreciative of their heroes;
they are sensual vixens; or they are older, domesticated, and
neither exciting nor very important. The good ones display the
virtues of prudence, courage, temperance, faith, and hope. The
neutral ones simply survive, fade into a gray background, and
arouse little reader interest. The villainesses display not only
pride in their beauty and wiliness, but also lust, terrible anger,
and occasional avarice. Few women in Short are charitable,
while none is gluttonous or slothful.

Short's good women may be tall or short, or in between, and

dark or fair; but to be good they must be patient and loyal. Chris Mellish (*Brand of Empire*) patiently nurses her Pete back to health, twice, and elects meanwhile to be loyal to him rather than to her own brother. Amy Lufton (*Gunman's Chance*) is more decent than her fiery sister Carol and, therefore, prospers in the end. Rose Leland (*Ramrod*) is maturely considerate and level-headed throughout her troubled time in the little town of Signal. Kate Hardison (*Coroner Creek*) and Jen Truro (*Paper Sheriff*), both saddled with crippled fathers,[14] endure and ultimately win out. Hearty Tess Falette is far cleverer at the game of survival than prim Carrie Tavister (*Fiddlefoot*). Carrie Bentall (*The Whip*) is wondrously stoical and is built to survive in an area she never sought to live in. Tenney Payne (*The Primrose Try*), Laurie Mays (*The Deserters*), and Stacey Wheelis (*The Man from Two Rivers*) do arduous domestic work cheerfully and with faith that times will improve.

To my mind, the three most compelling heroines in all of Short are Rose Leland, Carrie Bentall, and Jen Truro. Characteristics which they share are low-keyed common sense, a willingness to be just to—or perhaps only amiably tolerant of—opposing points of view, and a quiet courage to defy all odds. Here is Rose: "She turned to face him then, and smiled in friendly welcome. She was a girl of medium height, full bosomed, with pale hair so thick it was almost untidy. She was wearing an apron now over her house dress, and her ·sleeves were half rolled. Her mouth was full, friendly, and there was a humor in her brown eyes now as she regarded Dave, hands on hips" (pp. 6–7).[15] Here is Carrie:

Gannon looked around and saw a girl standing behind him, a beginning smile on her face. She was slim and could have been twenty, and the first thing Will noticed about her were her eyebrows winging thick and dark over pale green eyes. A mass of shiny chestnut hair was brushed cleanly away from her temples and was gathered by a ribbon at the base of her neck. Her grey dress, Will noted, was darned and patched but spotlessly clean, and there was a faint dusting of freckles across the bridge of her small nose. Her lips were full and, as her smile faded under Will's cool appraisal, they set in a sober self-assurance. (p. 7)

Finally, here is Jen, a lawyer in court: "She was watching him from wide-spaced eyes so black they were colorless. Her dark hair, a little dishevelled, framed a face that was now thoughtful and tired, holding a resignation that marred its almost classic beauty. She was dressed in a simple suit of dark grey with a white blouse underneath. She wore no jewelry. . ." (p. 5).

Other good women in Short include hotel workers, waitresses, newspaper women, doctors' wives or aides, storekeepers' helpers, housekeepers, teachers, landladies, and office secretaries and clerks. Many are simply passive widows, wives, or daughters. The position never demeans or glorifies; the innate qualities of the particular woman do so. The reward of feminine goodness is almost universally marriage to the hero, or at least aid from him in making good an escape to anonymous safety. Almost never is a good woman hurt long or punished much. Occasionally a merely tolerable woman, usually older and faded, is obliged by plot exigencies to suffer through obligatory association with a villain.

All of this may sufficiently suggest what is true, that heroines in Short's novels are as a rule unimportant. They usually exist to inspire heroes and be available as prizes.

But what of the villainesses? There are three genuinely evil women of major stature in Short. Their emergence predates the modern women's liberation movement by some years and perhaps shows that Short wanted to enrich his plots by stirring in the activities of a few heady bitches. The three are Connie Dickason (*Ramrod*), who hates her father, uses men, lies, and causes many deaths; Holly Heath (*Rimrock*), who is explicitly motivated by a desire to outdo men—at all costs—in mining, traditionally a male occupation; and Tina Bowers (*Three for the Money*), who combines a smoldering feline sexuality with murderous amorality. All such unbecoming, unfeminine conduct ends in grief.

Two other women in Short pose curious problems for the would-be analyst of their behavior. They are Carol Lufton (*Gunman's Chance*) and Callie Branham (*Paper Sheriff*). Neither is actively sinful so much as crazed by passion. Carol would do almost anything—even hurt the legitimate interests of her family—to please Tate Riling, her totally selfish lover. And Callie would do almost anything to hurt her good husband, Reese, whom she imagines to be faithless. Both misguided women are used by others worse than they. Both suffer, perhaps mainly because they wrenched the fabric of family life.

Short depicts two other women who fail to achieve his notion of womanly success, both for the same reason. Will Gannon's wife in *The Whip* has deserted him and run off to San Francisco and a rich cad, and in remorse commits suicide—an end which Short elsewhere reserves only for a few evil men. Sistie Cable in *Trouble Country* unpardonably lusts for the hero: "As she began to clean up[the kitchen] she thought again about Sam. He was a good man, she told herself—kind, knowledgeable, and, at long last, a steady man with property. He would, she thought, make a fine husband and father to the children she wanted." She overplays her hand, becomes sanctimonious and cruelly critical of an injured rival woman, and scares Sam off. So it quickly follows that "Sam looked at her carefully and read a cold, calculated anger in her always-pretty face. He thought, *This gal is a little bit crazy; none of what she's saying does she know to be true, only gossip, and intended to shame me!*" (pp. 58, 94).

It contributes to our understanding of women in Short to note that good men in his works do not act violently in front of women, and further that if a man is discourteous to a woman fate will deal harshly with him. When thick Sheriff Sam Kinsley (*Sunset Graze*) tries to stop Beth Hilliard from riding into an ongoing crossfire between ignorant townsmen and the hero, she only smiles, rides serenely on, and—we read—all "shooting. . . .ceased" (p. 144). Villainous Bill Taff (*High Vermilion*) says, " 'Shut up, Fatty' " (p. 46) to an admittedly monstrous hotel manageress; within three pages the hero has broken the discourteous man's nose and left him unconscious in vermilion mud outside. Worse, June Constable (*The Stalkers*) slugs his common-law wife and then impolitely labels her a " 'goddamn *idiot* sow!' " (p. 139). Eight pages later he lies dead.

CHAPTER 5

Short's Plots

IT was fairly easy to describe Luke Short's various settings and variety of characters. But it is more difficult to define his plot patterns. Three quite different critics provide categories into which we might place the plot situations of Short's novels, but none is especially helpful. Georges Polti's classic treatment, *The Thirty-Six Dramatic Situations*,[1] tempts us to conclude that Short's imaginative fertility was feeble. But if it was, then so was Zane Grey's and so is Louis L'Amour's — and so has been that of all other writers of Western fiction. Frank Gruber in *The Pulp Jungle* says that there are only seven basic Western plots, while William Wright in *Six Guns and Society*, although writing specifically only about Western movies, reductively divides all Western action into four varieties.

I   *Thirty-Six Plots?*

Clearly, most of Polti's thirty-six situations are irrelevant in the Far West, especially the way formulaic action there is handled by a writer as conservative as Short. Thus, we would not expect to find in Short's novels such dramatic situations as adultery, madness, or conflict with a god; further, certain other Polti categories, such as supplication, obtaining, and the discovery of the dishonor of a loved one, are rare in Short. In fact, he regularly employs only a few of Polti's defined situations; they are, in descending order of frequency, rivalry of superior and inferior, daring enterprise, crime pursued by vengeance, the enigma, falling prey to cruelty, and revolt. If Polti could have classified Short's plot situations, he would have regarded the novelist's actions as limited pretty much to armed conflict in connection with missions of rescue, vengeance, and justice.

II   *Seven Plots?*

Gruber is, as would be expected, more germane. Of his seven fundamental Western plots, Short illustrates five with great regularity. Here are Gruber's groups: (1) the Union Pacific Story, in which the hero builds something, in defiance of villains or stubborn nature; (2) the Ranch Story, which pits rivals seeking control of land; (3) the Empire Story, about the far-seeing exploiter of range land or a mine who seeks to hold his own and expand it in spite of oncoming opposition; (4) the Revenge Story, in which villainy is pursued and punished, and tranquility restored; (5) Custer's Last Stand, the age-old story of cowboys and/or cavalry versus Indians; (6) the Outlaw Story, which details the admirable reformation of a "bad man"; and (7) the Marshal Story, the epic of a lawman (or a military officer) who protects a town, a camp, and individuals from forces of evil.[2]

Naturally, all of Short's convoluted plots cross Gruber's neat lines of artificial demarcation. Thus, more than thirty of Short's novels may be called revenge stories, in which wrongdoers are hunted down, criminals punished, and victims of malevolence saved and restored to happiness. In fully half of Short's plots, ranchers fight to hold their land, cattlemen attempt to stem the tide of encroaching nesters, rustlers threaten to bleed off herds owned by pioneering cowmen, sheepmen clash with old-fashioned cattle herders, and roundup and trail bosses face perils both man-made and natural. In a dozen or so Short novels, we have variations on the Union Pacific Story—that is, honest freighters try to build their businesses, cowmen their herds, stagecoach operators their routes, miners their load of ore, homesteaders their shacks, and so on. Usually, such would-be builders oppose empire builders, either incipient or already arrived; therefore, the Union Pacific Story often overlaps the empire-builder tale, which by itself is not important in Short. Finally, he presents some ten stories of admirable law-and-order men. So, of Gruber's seven groups, Short illustrates five often; but he seldom uses the Outlaw Story and even more rarely uses what Gruber calls Custer's Last Stand.

The purest of Short's Union Pacific novels are *Dead Freight for Piute* and *The Whip;* the best ranch stories, *Ride the Man Down, Ramrod, And the Wind Blows Free,* and *Saddle by Starlight;* the

most obvious empire-builder tale, *Brand of Empire;* the starkest
revenge plots, those of *The Branded Man, War on the Cimarron,
Sunset Graze, Coroner Creek, Debt of Honor,* and *The Guns of
Hanging Lake;* the humblest variation of Custer's Last Stand,
Ambush; the best outlaw stories, *Bold Rider* and *Hardcase;* and
the most classic marshal stories, *Paper Sheriff, The Primrose Try,*
and *The Stalkers.*

III   *Four Plots?*

Wright divides all Western films into four types. First, in the
classical plot, the stranger rides into a troubled town and cleans
it up, thus winning the respect of the citizenry and meriting the
schoolmarm's love. Second, the vengeance variation has a hero
who is already a resident of the town, which is weak; the hero,
after the villain has harmed him (or the town), leaves on a
mission of punishment, succeeds, returns, and reenters society.
Third, the minor transitional theme, according to Wright, features a hero inside a strong society at first; he successfully fights
for justice but is then rejected by the townspeople, and leaves—
often in the company of an equally outraged heroine. Fourth, the
professional plot gives us a gunfighter hero outside society and
fighting ominous villains—but only because it is his paid job to do
so, and because it is also challenging and fun.[3]
Short frequently illustrates the classic plot. Well over half of
his novels present heroes who are strangers to the community at
first, are not completely accepted, are often reluctantly drawn
into conflict initially involving villain versus society, and yet
eventually emerge triumphant, applauded, and accepted. Many
examples could be cited. In *Coroner Creek,* the hero though a
stranger is not around too long in the town of Triumph before his
special abilities are so noted by the sheriff that he is made
deputy. And in *Man from the Desert,* the hero enters Kittrick to
expose the corrupt town banker, does so while under a cloud of
suspicion himself part of the time, but marries there.
The vengeance variation is one which Short uses well. *King
Colt* is a good example, but also a poor novel. A near-perfect
example is *The Guns of Hanging Lake,* in the course of which the
hero not only leaves to accomplish his purpose but dragoons the
alcoholic deputy sheriff to go along and connive illegally in the
process.

Short avoids the transition theme almost completely. It is too innovative to appeal to a popular writer reluctant to deviate from his successful patterns. However, we do find the hero of *Play a Lone Hand* at the end anxious to shake the dust of Corazon from his heels, and to gallop off with the heroine.[4]

Wright's final category, the professional plot, is exemplified a few times in Short, mostly in novels written after the midpoint of his career. Thus the heroes of *Desert Crossing* and *Three for the Money*, among other good heroes, are motivated by professional pride and the unsentimental desire for monetary reward.[5]

IV *A Thousand Faces?*

Short offers considerably more variety than makers of formulaic Western films. So a more fruitful way of displaying motifs in his novels may be through seeing their resemblance to aspects of folktale, legend, and myth. With some slight adjustment in our thinking, does not the following critical statement sound like a description of Short's works? "Everything is clear. . . . We know exactly where to place our sympathy. The issues are soon stated, with no unnecessary subtleties of emotion, no bewildering wavering between cause and effect. Everyone acts in character, and the stories move in strong, direct action to the always expected end, where the good come to glory and joy, and evil is punished, as befits it, with primitive symbols of suffering." The improbable source of this quotation is an introductory section of a standard anthology of children's literature. The ellipsis dots replace "in the folktale."[6]

Joseph Campbell is even more helpful. In his monumental *Hero with a Thousand Faces,*[7] he offers a subtle summary of the composite hero's adventures in world-wide myths, legends, fairy tales, folklore, and religions. Campbell suggests that the hero is enticed, is forced, or volunteers to move from familiar terrain to "the threshold of adventure," where he confronts a passageway guardian, whom he defeats or mollifies, or is temporarily defeated by. Then follows progress "through a world of unfamiliar yet strangely intimate forces," which may threaten or help him. In either case, the hero descends to "the nadir of the mythological round," endures a climactic ordeal, and gains a reward—the love of a female, recognition by a father figure, or a rare "apotheosis." It is frequent, however, for the hero sadly to lose his reward, and thereafter become wiser, sadder, freer. Finally, he returns, either protected by "the powers" or harried by adversaries. Regardless, at the end he "re-emerges from the kingdom of dread" and "restores the world" (pp. 245, 256).

We can easily translate this rather lofty language, which is suitable to describe the plots of Classical and Romantic legends, into more prosaic lingo appropriate to a discussion of Short's main actions. If his composite hero does not have a thousand faces, he does have half a hundred; and, although he is never dismembered, carried off in a whale's belly, bereft of his elixir, or given in sacred marriage to a goddess, still—again, in humbler terms—he does ring changes on a number of episodic elements in the cycle which Campbell diagrams and elucidates.[8]

Just as Aristotle in his *Poetics* explains that the plot of a Greek tragic drama must have a beginning, a middle, and an end, so Campbell divides his composite plot line into three parts, which he calls departure, initiation, and return.[9]

V   *Departure*

The call to adventure is sounded in Short in several ways. Shamrock Ireland (*The Man on the Blue*), running away from the law, gallops straight into a strange scene: a girl on a horse has roped a man and is dragging him toward some rocks. Shamrock instantly cuts her lariat, and the plot opens. Webb Cousins (*Marauders' Moon*) is more passively introduced to the action. He is being brought into Wagon Mound by a sheriff as a falsely accused suspect in a robbery. Suddenly five robbers explode on the scene and kill the sheriff, whereupon the local lawman, his hands full, releases Webb into the custody of one of a pair of feuding ranchers. Webb must take sides. Dave Nash (*Ramrod*), his wife and more recently his little boy dead, drifts into a new town, drinks too much, and is abortively befriended by a man whose cowardice and then escape leave a power vacuum into which Dave is drawn. Tully Gibbs (*Silver Rock*) happens to learn through his disliked radarman in Korea of a rich mine back in the States, and thus his adventures and regeneration begin.

Some Short heroes are reluctant and initially decline the call to action. But not many behave this way for long. And they always change their minds. At first, even before *The Man from Two Rivers* starts, Hobe Carew had been run off his own land by forces superior in strength to his own. In the first chapter of *Bold Rider,* Poco St. Vrain refuses to listen to Two-Way Hornbeck's scheme, which later lures him into legend-making activity. Keefe Calhoun (*Summer of the Smoke*) tries to stay strictly neutral in the dust-up between the army and the Apaches, since wrongful actions on both sides have turned a region he loves into a waste land. Sometimes it is dangerous to be deaf to adventure's siren voice, as Jim Donovan (*Donovan's Gun*) learns when he prefers his law office to either side in a local feud between ranchers and squatters.[10] Often in folklore we find brother against brother, and twice in Short half-brothers clash terribly (*First Campaign* and *Trouble Country*). Consideration for the father (or father figure) acts as a temporary restraint (*Vengeance Valley*). Sometimes a victim is so benighted as to refuse rescue (*Paper Sheriff*).

But once the hero is in motion toward adventuresome deeds, he finds that fate usually favors him so spectacularly that even in Short's realistic plots it seems not extravagant to define that aid as "supernatural" (Campbell, p. 69). Thus, Pete Yard (*Brand of Empire*), though tortured, mends miraculously under the ministrations of doctor and nurse. Jim Wade (*Savage Range*) finds a herculean assistant in Jack Cope, who is introduced in epical terms:

He was a mountain of a man, his bones smothered in great folds of flesh that caricatured every line of him. . . . Jim saw that his right leg was gone, the empty trouser leg pinned up. A thick oak crutch was propped under his arm, and he strangely contrived to move with an agility which was as swift as it was ponderous. He shouldered a loafer out of his way, sending him spinning, and then he plowed into a handful of men. . . . They parted for him, and he stopped under the lamp, his shaven head round and set stubbornly on his shoulders and beaded with a fine sweat. (p. 17)

As mentioned earlier, Tip Woodring (*Bounty Guns*) obtains more advice than he can at first handle from oracle-like Uncle Dave Shawn, who enigmatically intones the names of friends and foes with sibyllic dispassion. In *Sunset Graze* and *Coroner Creek*, men whose real identities are unknown to the heroes work silently for their betterment. Further, the near-magic, Indian-like tracking ability of old Ives the wolfer (*Sunset Graze*), and the almost superhuman skill of Running Bear (*The Some-Day Country*) and the half-breed Jim Byers (*The Man from Two Rivers*), are virtual guarantees of their heroic friends' success.

Campbell figuratively describes the start of the typical hero's tough adventure as "the crossing of the first threshold" (p. 77). In Short, the threshold is often the literal one of a saloon. Over and over again, his heroes shoulder past saloon batwings which separate the relatively safe street outside and mystery in the murky, cavelike interior. His heroes typically let their eyes adjust to the darkness of this new world, challenge the cruising, cue-armed housemen, and penetrate to the recesses where the action is. Thus, John Haven (*Station West*) strides into the Prince Marion saloon, sloshes wine on part-owner Mick Marion, a veritable Minotaur of a man, and soon beats him up—to gain respect and start the action. Similarly, Pete Brisbin (*The Deserters*) brawls in villainous Ben Maule's Crossfire saloon: Pete beards the lion in his den, eyes his neck-scarred mistress Lace Ferrill, challenges his henchmen, and escapes to a sanctuary provided by the heroine—all in one smooth early sequence which brilliantly overtures all later action.

Once the hero is committed to his adventure, he experiences a kind of shaking off of part of his old identity, profits by a change in his nature often tediously known as a rebirth, and continues along his path to action. Some heroes even take new names for a while: Poco St. Vrain (*Bold Rider*) becomes Jake Finger; Pete Yard (*Brand of Empire*), Welch; Sam Teacher (*Bought with a Gun*), Jim Melody; Tim Sefton (*The Stalkers*), Jim Battles, Hal Simons, and the Professor; and so on. As for rebirth symbolism, the miraculous rope by which the heroine brings Poco up to life again out of the valley beyond the cliff is surely umbilical. And Dave Coyle's rebirth early in his story is imaged by his popping out of a coffin in a train baggage car.

VI   *Initiation*

New challenges confront the hero once he commits himself to his course of action. In the Western version of the ageless adventure yarn, he is shot, stabbed, burned, dragged, frozen, and rained on; and he wears himself down by galloping great distances with little or no rest. An early test for passive Joel Hardy (*And the Wind Blows Free*) is a cold, four-day plunge by stage along the Chisholm Trail deep into Indian territory. A later test for Joel's *beau ideal* Jim Wade is the days-long fight to extinguish a prairie fire. Jim and his men control the fire in part by the epic device of slaughtering steers, splitting their carcasses, and dragging them belly down along the fire edge.

Silence, loneliness, and a thinning-down effect often accompany the hero on his "road of trials" (Campbell, p. 97). For example, when Dave Wallace (*Sunset Graze*) prepares to lead pursuit astray so that his cohorts can seek vital evidence, he observes that "off to the south was the vast spread of reservation grassland, while to the west lay the big and silent desert. Something of the loneliness of both was on this land." After his ordeal, he rejoins a companion; and ". . .Pete had a look at him. Dave's face told the whole story of these past few days. A black beard stubble blurred the sharp planes of his face but could not hide the gaunted cheeks or his sunken eyes. Salt from dried sweat faintly crusted his thick eyebrows" (pp. 114, 136). Heroic journeys purify heroes.

The important women whom Short's men encounter are mainly either helpful or tempting. The former conform to aspects of Campbell's "goddess"; the latter, those of his "temptress" (pp. 109, 120). Since Westerns have little room for female complexities, we are right if we expect Short's works to provide little evidence for the likes of Campbell to elaborate upon. Short's goddesses are varied but are often similar in function with, respect to the heroes. Mary Buckner (*Savage Range*) at first is aloof, coolly beautiful, almost divine in Wade's smitten eyes; he pledges himself, like a knight, to fight in her cause.[11] Crippled Mrs. Grady Sebree, who appears only once in *Play a Lone Hand*, arms Giff against her hated husband by pointing him toward damning evidence. Cornelia Traver, rape victim in *Debt of Honor*, is an aging semi-divinity to whom Reeves willingly plays acolyte: "She had always been a beautiful woman and still was, Reeves thought, and time had not smothered that look of vitality she had always seemed to radiate" (p. 7).

Short's temptresses are harder to comment on than his goddesses. If the temptress is older, she is almost always spurned, no matter how attractive. Take, for example, Vannie Shore in *Hard Money*. Although she has provided Phil Seay with track for the mine and is rich and "widowed," and although her sensuality perfumes and drugs the night near him, she is not pure like

Sharon and is hence replaced. Vannie gives him up with a sigh:
" 'You are full of her, Phil. Well, go on, and God bless you, you
poor fool. And when you know her, Phil, and if it isn't too late, I'll
be here' " (p. 88). But Vannie waits in vain.

Short's gallery includes other temptresses who fail. Josephine
Storrs (*High Vermilion*), ravishingly beautiful and young enough,
is a loser like Vannie, because she married a loser and goes down
with him. Lottie Priest (*Ride the Man Down*) loses the hero
because she is timid and materialistic, and also because she tries
to tell him what to think and do. Della Harms (*Coroner Creek*) is
anemically tempting; Chris Danning ramrods for her but finally
rejects her since although "she seemed somehow appealing" she
is "without iron, without stability, impetuous one moment, sorry
for what her impetuosity had cost her the next" (pp. 139, 140).
Kate Hardison in the same novel is a counterpoise to Della; Kate
warns the villain that she will kill him if he injures Chris. She is
not very ladylike in traditional Short terms. But then neither is
Tess Falette (*Fiddlefoot*), who in addition to being beautiful
(". . .she lent a kind of splendor to this drab [accounting] room"
[p. 4]) plays poker with the men. As a contrast to Tess in the
same novel is Carrie Tavister, who is the daughter of the local
judge, as well as Frank Chess's too-patient, untempting fiancée.
She calls Frank " 'son' " (pp. 14, 129, 130), does not want him to
kick her flowerpots, hates to see his horse nibble her front lawn,
and obviously must lose him.

A curious pair of temptresses are minor characters Julie Sands
(*Raiders of the Rimrock*) and Selena Cosby (*Last Hunt*). Julie has
been turned into a man-hating zombie by her villainous father,
but the dogged devotion of gunslinger St. Cloud finally touches
her humanity. Selena runs off with her sheriff husband's
infatuated deputy, but the reader has every reason to believe
that their misconduct will ultimately satisfy neither.[12]

Of the few prostitutes in Short's fiction, only Pony Mortensen
(*Debt of Honor*) is treated in the round. After she and injured
Reeves have befriended each other, she offers to spend the night
with him there in his hotel room—" 'For free. . . .' " He says
that the management might object, but the reader may suspect
that he is gentle in declining temptation mainly because he has
planted Beth Fanning in the room closet to eavesdrop. The girl
soon emerges, and—we read—"In contrast with Pony, she
looked like a nun" (pp. 66, 67). Beth may be from the naive East,

but she makes a knowledgeable comment about women, when, earlier, she says: " 'You don't understand much about women, do you, Reeves? They were born to take care of dull and dirty business. . .' " (p. 53).

The father figures in Short's novels are numerous when we gather them together. They are usually surrogates, since almost without exception the heroes are orphans. Typical of our orphan heroes are Will Ballard (*Ride the Man Down*), Lee McPhail (*Last Hunt*), Reeves Cable (*Debt of Honor*), Hal Hanaway (*Man from the Desert*), and Will Christie (*The Outrider*). Details do not vary much. When McPhail was ten years old, his father died in a railroad accident; a little later, while fishing, the youth met Judge John Lillard, who taught him the art of dry-fly casting,[13] gave him a fly rod and its accoutrements, and thus initiated "a strange companionship that blossomed thereafter." At vacation time during his later college years, made possible by the influential and well-to-do judge, "the Lillard house was a second home" to Mac (p. 37). As far as he is concerned, the judge's murder cost him a true father.[14] Hal Hanaway midway through *Man from the Desert* breaks open his youthful memories during a picnic with Carrie Kittrick: orphaned at seven, taken in by a lawyer uncle whose example was not inspiring, Hal soon became "a complete drifter" until Jeff Kittrick, Carrie's now dead uncle, befriended the youth, hired him at roundup time, paid him off in beef, and sold him land enough to strike out "on his own. He was through being a saddle tramp" (p. 80). No wonder Hal answers Carrie's plea to her uncle for help: Hal becomes surrogate to a surrogate. Similarly, Will Christie explains his background to an almost identically sympathetic heroine: "In answer to Belle's gentle questioning he said that he could only barely remember his mother and his father, who had died of smallpox on a cattle-buying trip to Mexico" (p. 57). No wonder Joe Isom, the crusading lieutenant governor, becomes Christie's role model. Further, at the end, we know that Belle's father, Brady Cope, will be yet another substitute father for the hero-in-law.[15]

Most interestingly, one Short hero invents a father for himself to enable him to get in with a criminal gang in spite of his evident schooling. "His story was that he was the runaway son of a revivalist preacher and had dedicated most of his short life so far to breaking every moral rule his father believed in" (*The Primrose Try*, p. 39).[16]

It is of incidental interest that fathers of women in Short are usually dead, are sometimes crippled, and only rarely prove to be of much help. Thus magnificent Carrie Bentall (*The Whip*) is fatherless, the crippled fathers of Kate Hardison (*Coroner Creek*) and Jen Truro (*Paper Sheriff*) place demands on their dutiful offspring, and Ty Hoad, the weak father of Callie Branham (*Paper Sheriff* again), actually encourages his daughter to break the law, and worse. Only big, rumpled Dr. Channon, of all Short's fathers of daughters, is whole and admirable; he advises his daughter Abby in *Rimrock* in the good old-fashioned way: Marry the guy.

The celebrated apotheosis, standard in myth, is minimal in Short, whose heroes, after confronting goddesses and temptresses, and after coming to terms with father figures, spend little time being compassionate, conciliatory, forgiving, and peaceful. Instead, they rush on toward the next step in the basic plot pattern, which is to gain evidence leading to the putting down of evil. This "ultimate boon" (Campbell, p. 172) takes the form in Short of an awareness of gold or other precious metal or coal, or the recovery (or preservation) of the amuletlike goods—that is, identifiable weapons, a key chain, pieces of clothing, spurs, and especially incriminating papers. One of the creakiest aspects of Short's fiction is what may be called the missing-deed gimmick. Short uses it too frequently.

VII   *Return*

Short's heroes never refuse to return and to face the climax. John Haven (*Station West*) may be reluctant to tell Mary Iles the truth about her fiancé, but he would ruthlessly destroy him to get into the enemy stronghold, except that an assistant kills the sinner first. Ward Kinsman (*Ambush*) withdraws from the fight in the desert between the army and Diablito's Apaches; but he soon thinks more realistically about his responsibility, scouts some more, returns to report, and fights on to success. Jim Donovan (*Donovan's Gun*) manfully resists the temptation to join the Hethridges against the squatters, or even those nesters against the Hethridges. But eventually he is drawn into the ranch war, which then races like a burning fuse to its fatal explosion. The best example of the temporarily reluctant hero in Short is old-fashioned Hal Hanaway, whom halfway through *Man from the Desert* the author depicts as wanting to ride away from it all. Hal thinks that his work in the hated town of Kittrick is done and further that Carrie Kittrick, enticing though she is, would prove incompatible: "She'd been brought up in luxury and had money of her own. How could he take her north to his modest and isolated spread? She was a town girl" (p. 98). But love finds a way.[17]

The rush toward the climax in a typical Short novel is unabated. The hero is spurred on by twin desires, revenge and love. He regularly has a sturdy horse to help him. Shamrock Ireland (*The Man on the Blue*) clearly has the finest; in fact, man and horse are subtly equated early in the novel: "He swung lazily onto the blue [horse], settled the old and battered Stetson more securely over his blue-black hair, and. . ." (p. 8). In addition, the typical Short hero is a fine tracker. The best example is Will Gannon (*The Whip*), who not only pursues a pair of canny killers, one of whom is part Indian, but actually anticipates their moves, parallels their route ahead of them, and springs an ambush upon them.

Preclimactic rescues are often managed by outside help, sometimes of an almost miraculous nature. Rarely does the army come to the rescue, but in varying degrees of efficiency it is permitted to do so in *Brand of Empire, Station West, Desert Crossing*, and *The Deserters*. On the other hand, the army is worse than useless in *War on the Cimarron, And the Wind Blows Free*, and *Summer of the Smoke*. Once in a while, the sluggish law steps in and, as we have partly seen, bails out the oppressed, stymied, or temporarily immobilized hero, as in *Raw Land, Hardcase, Trouble Country*, and especially *Man from the Desert*. But usually, if the hero cannot manage by himself, it is a friend who intervenes privately. Such aides, all variously prejudiced, are Red Schibe (*War on the Cimarron*), Pearly Gates (*Bought with a Gun*), Mead Calhan (*Vengeance Valley*), Benjy Schell (*The Guns of Hanging Lake*), and Dr. Rob Hasketh (*The Stalkers*). A few times, because of plot exigencies, the hero needs massive outside help. For example, since Reese Branham (*Paper Sheriff*) cannot be expected to kill, or even to arrest, his cattle-rustlin' wife, Short ingeniously has the murder of an outside trail boss by her depraved uncle bring in some Texans who are cronies of the victim. Mrs. Branham is caught in the ultimate crossfire. She has been cavorting around in her husband's turned-up trousers; so what does she expect?

Older women sometimes aid the hero, often at considerable personal cost to themselves. Thus, over-the-hill Belle Weymarn (*Summer of the Smoke*), slatternly wife of the villain, does not tell her husband when Keefe Calhoun finds the dead soldier's uniform hidden in Weymarn's storeroom. Further, she later alerts Keefe to the presence in town of her husband's fast gunman—thus saving the hero's life. Admittedly, Belle is irate that her husband lied to her; but in Short's novels lies are rarely a cause for profound moral censure. At least once, an older woman unwittingly aids the hero through selfishly beseeching him for help. Lace Ferrill (*The Deserters*), when she asks Pete to take her by buggy away from villainous Ben Maule, whose mistress and indeed whose chattel she is, helps precipitate the final clever action which is ruinous to Ben.[18]

Short's heroes cross "the return threshold" (Campbell, p. 217) with uncommon speed. That is, once they have the damaging evidence in hand, they can call the villain out to the walkdown— or any of its well-staged equivalents—with a minimum of words and a maximum of violence. The final action is good force against evil; and in Short's works and in other stories of the folktale formula—if not in life—good is always glorified and evil always toppled. For the most representative examples among fifty-one, Cole Armin presents all pertinent damning evidence to his supposed uncle, challenges him, and in the ensuing rolling brawl chokes him to death (*Dead Freight for Piute*); Sam Teacher, in a folklore finale, blows Santee Bales off a mountain rim to his death three hundred feet below (*Bought with a Gun*); and Dave Coyle, in a sequence of the sort immortalized on a million feet of Hollywood celluloid, blasts his enemy out a window, down a roof, and so on "dully to the ground, like a sack of dropped oats" (*Hardcase*, p. 164).

In many of Short's novels written after World War II, the villains are killed by the hero's proxy, so to speak. Such is the case in *Summer of the Smoke, Vengeance Valley, The Guns of Hanging Lake, Man from the Desert, The Man from Two Rivers,* and *Trouble Country.* It almost seems as though Short is tardily saying, with Hemingway, that a man alone, no matter how far west and no matter how tough, ain't got no chance.

In some cases, again in later works, evildoers are arrested instead of being killed, and will face later trial and perhaps execution. Examples occur in *Station West, Last Hunt, The Deserters,* and *Three for the Money.* In a couple of cases, shadowy villains in the obscure background, after nominal exposure, survive to carry on, although their gun-wielding subordinates hit the dust. For example, Chris Feldhake dies but his boss, Servel Janeece, evidently lives on, almost like an immortal spider (*Hard Money*); and Hugh Ganley escapes the entire region polluted by his gunslinging hired nesters (*Saddle by Starlight*). Once, in a curious violation of the formula, a hired murderer kills and escapes, while his less muscular employer is shot to death by the hero (*Debt of Honor*).

Short speeds each climax so breathtakingly that his typical denouement follows by a page or two, if that, and then the book slaps shut. Usually the very final action is "bang, bang, kiss, kiss"—which sounds a little like a reversal of the title of Pauline Kael's partly inept book on movies, including Westerns (*Kiss Kiss Bang Bang*, 1968). We may assume that by the end Short's heroes have developed an ability to be "master of the two worlds" (Campbell, p. 229)—one being the violence-cured present, and the other the amorous tomorrow. For a few examples among many, the hero of *Marauders' Moon* survives to marry a young woman who has returned to her senses and who has a splendid if crotchety father. The hero of *Raiders of the Rimrock* saves the region from sheepherders, inherits a ranch from a surrogate father, and plans to wed a cooperative neighbor. The same, almost, is true of the hero of *Vengeance Valley,* except that the surrogate father is still living.

Marriage gives Short's heroes a surprising number of parents-in-law, usually one each, but far more often old fathers-in-law. Note such a consequence of wedding bells in *War on the Cimarron, Gunman's Chance, Station West, High Vermilion, Rimrock, Desert Crossing,* and *The Outrider.* For a rarity, Belle Cope (*The Outrider*) is a heroine (though a minor one) with both parents living. Almost as though to try to hold to his pattern, Short keeps Belle's mother back home on the upstate ranch, away from all action in and around corrupt Granite Forks. Juliana Frost (*Desert Crossing*) is going to join both of her parents at Fort Whipple, but neither parent appears in the novel.

Short endows few of his heroines with living mothers. Women

regularly died early in the Far West. Aptly enough, therefore, Short populates only *Silver Rock, The Primrose Try,* and *The Guns of Hanging Lake* with heroines' mothers who actively participate in events. The first is a peppy librarian who enjoys an occasional drink; the second is thoroughly friendly; and the third is properly cowed by novel's end. So the respective heroes need anticipate no *belle mère* difficulties. (Only in *Saddle by Starlight* does a heroine seek and presumably get to keep a surrogate mother.)

If freedom in the West is freedom to leave the scene of gloomy action, then a few of Short's heroes are free at the end of their respective trials. Thus the lovers in *The Some-Day Country* are free to try a life together as far as possible from the discredited Boomers. Further, the happy pair in *Three for the Money* can return to the hero's now solvent ranch up north near Cow Springs, which we readers have not had the pleasure of even glimpsing. Best expressed is Giff Dixon's invitation to his bride-to-be to go with him at novel's end to " 'a place in Wyoming way back against the peaks. I've passed it [he continues] a dozen times. It's so far back from a town it's lost. We'll have to build a school for our kids' " (*Play a Lone Hand*, p. 152). Somewhat similarly, Reeves and Beth want "[t]heir children. . .[to] be raised away from festering towns like this [Primrose]" (*Debt of Honor*, p. 128). Even better, perhaps, because they are even more innocent, Will Danning and Becky Case in *Raw Land* deliberately keep themselves ignorant that there is copper on his land and agree to leave the region together without finding out what the squads of opposing villains have been fighting over.

It may seem petty to conclude on a critical note. However, it is true that two of Short's novels end somewhat unsatisfactorily, and the Western formula would seem to require things to wind up otherwise. First, *And the Wind Blows Free*, which had the potential to be a novel quite distinct from Short's more nearly predictable ones, concludes with the formerly frustrated lovers together at last, in a wintry scene of devastation, death, and bankruptcy perhaps appropriate for its unconsciously symbolic bleakness: since the two have failed separately, may we not legitimately predict that they will fail together in the future? Second, *The Whip* concludes with a firm-minded heroine—one of Short's most forthright and determined—abandoning her disapproval of Western-style violence and accepting as a husband a man half again her age and one of the most violent in all of Short.[19] He undoubtedly thought that the first of these troublesome novels ends happily, whereas it is more nearly pathetic, and that the second is a dark comedy, whereas it should have been made to conclude as tragedy.

CHAPTER 6

Short's Themes

ALMOST every novel, no matter how exclusively entertaining it aims to be, has a dominant theme.[1] The works of Luke Short are no exception. Obviously his primary purpose in writing was to be a best-selling novelist, by appealing to the love of vicarious Western adventure in millions of readers who dreamed of the Old West. But in the process he holds up a mirror to a way of life which has almost completely vanished and to a time when men were bold and self-reliant, when their word was their bond, when it was legitimate to wipe enemies' sneers from their faces with fists or bullets, when your property was yours if you were willing to fight for it, and when women knew their place and both thought and spoke pretty much the way their men encouraged them to—since men knew best.

What can Short's novels tell us to make us better and wiser? Perhaps not very much. But if we read several of them, we may well return to our own world a little more traditionally American, in the sense that we walk softly, carry a big stick, aid our friends and those less stalwart than ourselves, are courteous to all women, pay for what we break,[2] and even are constructively self-critical.

I *Titles*

Short's titles are usually a giveaway as to what he regards as of primary importance in his works. Most of his titles hint at action rather than characterization; others identify, however loosely, central characters more than they do locales. Thus Short, if his titles are informative, tells us that doing is more important than being, and that what we do is more important than where we do it. Action may grow out of setting in Short; but he subordinates place, if not person, to vital activity. So we have such titles as *The Feud at Single Shot, War on the Cimarron, Bought with a Gun,*

Barren Land Showdown, Ambush, Desert Crossing, Last Hunt,
and *Debt of Honor.* Each title alerts the reader to the likelihood
that action lies in wait for him—shooting, demanding, and
repaying. True, place names such as Single Shot and the
Cimarron appear; but with a minimum of rewriting in the two
texts, the following revised titles would be appropriate enough:
War at Single Shot and *The Feud along the Cimarron.*

Many of Short's titles center on the hero in such a way as to
suggest the type of action he will be in; thus we have *Bold Rider,*
Ramrod, Paper Sheriff, and *The Outrider.* The purpose of the
stories in *Hardcase* and *Fiddlefoot* is to show that, by heroic
action, persons who have been stigmatized can change.

Many titles center on locales, often hinting that they are
regions of deadly conflict. For example, we have *Savage Range*
and *Raw Land,*[3] *Coroner Creek, Vengeance Valley,* and *Trouble
Country.* Thus even when the title concerns a place, its purpose
is to lure the reader into an action story.

Most of Short's titles are good ones. Several are hauntingly
poetic. Only a few seem poor and even misleading.[4] Consider
these suggestive samples: *Brand of Empire* alerts us to watch for
the fall of a sagebrush Caesar; *Summer of the Smoke* warns us of
smoke signals on the horizon and hence probable trouble with
Indians; *Paper Sheriff* almost certainly implies that a nominal
lawman will turn real; *Three for the Money* not only suggests a
competitive search for loot but even hints at a less than grisly
tone in the narration of that search; and *The Stalkers* perhaps
tells the ingenious that one pursuer may be in danger of
becoming the pursued.[5] Short rarely wastes words to wax poetic
over his settings, but the following titles may hint that his West
was a land of muscular lyricism, all the same: *Marauders' Moon,*
*Raiders of the Rimrock, Ride the Man Down, And the Wind
Blows Free,* and *Saddle by Starlight.*

Always, however, the stress is on action. The implicit moral in
Short's collected titles is surely that life is motion, struggle,
change.

II *Themes in General*

The most frequently dramatized theme in Short's fiction is the
importance of obtaining justice, sometimes through gaining
evidence to put away a malefactor legally, usually through
wreaking simple violent vengeance on him. Next most often,

Short treats the theme of loyalty—dutifully riding hard, straight shooting for the man or the outfit that pays for your grub, or, if you are the boss, safeguarding your men the best way you can. Short also dramatizes the rightness of protecting women in the harsh West.

After these three themes, which are often intertwined into the body of a single novel, come three others less frequently employed but still central. They are the necessity of burying the dead and allaying old ghosts, the value of self-examination and self-reform, and the ecstasy of finding joy without directly seeking it.

In addition, three minor themes, which are never presented directly or importantly, are the contrast of West and East, the claim that a worthy end justifies—indeed, often requires—tawdry means, and the habitual defeat of mob action by rugged individualism.

Short's best novels have two or more major themes each. For example, *Coroner Creek* tells us about a man who is seeking revenge for the murder of his fiancée, is loyal to his two female employers and to his fellow workers in the strange region into which his search has led him to his quarry, bumps into a loving replacement for his earlier girl without taking time from his gory mission to seek one at all, and thus shelves the memory of his lost love. *Saddle by Starlight* is as complex: its hero is loyal to his widowed employer, sees to the security of a fine young woman who later replaces his uppity fiancée when she wrongly rejects him, and finds happiness with the worthier woman even though the novel opens on a scene in which he violently evicts her along with her no-good brother from squatted-on land.

Like most writers of Westerns, Short is limited in thematic range and ingenuity. So when he writes a novel with only breakneck action to sustain it and little in the way of a serious message, it does not rank high in his canon. Several of his novels are exciting but not memorable because they do not combine enough of his basic themes, the way his best ones do. Thus, *The Branded Man* is a simple story of revenge, of the efforts of a man to clear his dead brother's name. In *Savage Range,* a woman enlists the hero in her fight for justice over stolen land. *Raw Land* concerns little but admirable if misplaced loyalty. The *hero of Fiddlefoot* too suddenly sees his past for what it is, shameful, and proceeds to reform and seek justice, although he himself has unclean hands. *Ambush* is exciting as adventure but is thematically trivial. And so on.

III *Justice, Revenge*

In virtually every one of Short's novels, a villain has perpetrated or perpetrates a crime or a sin, and the mission of the hero is to see to it that the offender is punished. Sometimes the hero is an arm of the law and tries to operate within legal limits. Thus Tim Enever (*Raiders of the Rimrock*) enters the scene as a range detective, encounters the villainous sheepman Warner Sands in the first chapter, but knocks him out only to escape from him, to join forces with the good cattle people, and to defeat the enemy by at least quasi-legal means. In *Station West*, the hero, John Haven, is an undercover infantry lieutenant whose mission may be to recover stolen army uniforms but who must use information obtained by devious means in such a way as not to discredit his legal authority. Lieutenant Scott Milham (*The Some-Day Country*) dresses as a civilian but follows explicit orders from his commanding officer when he tracks the villain and his kidnap victim into Kansas.

Two of the best examples of lawmen operating within the spirit if not always within the letter of the law are the heroes of the back-to-back novels *Paper Sheriff* and *The Primrose Try*. In the former, a sheriff is hamstrung by having to seek proof, against massed villains, which will professionally satisfy the female attorney he loves. In the latter, the hero goes undercover and may be rough around the edges; but always he seeks facts which will stand up in court. The former novel begins with a murderer released after a joke trial,[6] and it ends with that villain shot dead. The latter novel begins with a murder; it too ends with villainy tricked and gory justice done.

The Deserters combines ingredients from *Station West*, *The Some-Day Country*, and *The Primrose Try:* in it an undercover military man moves over strange terrain to seek a foul murderer. His mode of operation is crude: he persuades the unsuspecting villain to name him sheriff of the town the villain has bought and now runs. This deputizing of the hero is not unique in Short, who also uses the device in *Bounty Guns*, *Coroner Creek*, and *Donovan's Gun*, among a few other novels. Finally, we have Will Christie (*The Outrider*) and Tim Sefton (*The Stalkers*): the

former, appointed by the state attorney general, enacts the role
of range outrider; however, he seeks not enemies of his
employer's stock of cattle, but rather those who enrich
themselves by suborning politicians. The latter, like Sam
Kennery of *The Primrose Try*, is yet another undercover deputy
seeking to destroy a nest of criminals, including a murderer.

Justice obtained by the ingenuity of lawmen, detectives,
undercover agents, and their sort, all operating pretty much
within the law, is all well and good, especially in real life. But in a
Western novel, the battered hero who reacts to injustice and sets
out to get revenge is more compelling. Thus the heroes of *Bounty
Guns, Dead Freight for Piute, Ride the Man Down, Play a Lone
Hand, The Guns of Hanging Lake,* and *Man from the Desert* are
all pretty much minding their own business until they get drawn
into unsought controversy and swing into swift action. Often the
law is so sluggish or corrupt that those heroes must take it into
their own hands or it will perish.

Occasionally a central character in a Short novel knows both
sides in a local or regional dispute, tries to mind his own business
and avoid getting involved, but is drawn into the deadly
squabble. Examples include the heroes of *Bought with a Gun,
Gunman's Chance, Ambush, Vengeance Valley, Play a Lone
Hand, The Whip, Summer of the Smoke, The Some-Day Country,*
and *Donovan's Gun.* Keefe Calhoun (*Summer of the Smoke*) and
Jim Donovan (*Donovan's Gun*) try, respectively, not to take
either side in an Apache versus army fight, and a rancher-nester
fight. Keefe scouts for the army; but, since he respects the
Apache way of life and also believes in fair play, he fires a
warning shot, during one assignment, to alert an Apache camp to
a sneak attack planned by American soldiers. This action starts
the avalanche of events which follows. Donovan wants nothing
so much as to practice law and run his little ranch; but during a
town dance he comes to the aid of Will-John Seton to prevent his
being bushwhacked by the nesters, and diabolical Will-John
assures Donovan's continued involvement by burning his ranch
and blaming the nesters. This two-pronged plot element impels
Donovan toward what may better be called revenge than
jurisprudence.

Short takes pains on occasion to point out that his good
characters are not totally good and his bad ones are what they
are in part because of unique Western circumstances. Thus, early

in *Ride the Man Down*, the weak owner of vast cattle lands, built up ruthlessly by his more violent brother, now dead, is willing to let his now stronger neighbor "steal" his land by pushing herds onto it. The weak man's foreman, hero Will Ballard, wants to fight for what his boss's family wrested from nature and weaker rivals in the first place. Hence the novel dramatizes a conflict between opponents defined in the first chapter as both partly in the wrong. Likewise, in the first chapter of *The Some-Day Country*, Short makes it clear that Oklahoma land is being contended for by Boomers prematurely invading it to homestead and villainous cowboys illegally "leasing" it for graze from ignorant Cheyenne-Arapaho Indians supposedly on nearby reservations, where justice would surely say they never should have been placed. A peace-in-our-time lawman comments unjudgmentally in one novel to this effect: " 'Hell, open range is for the man that can hold it' " (*Donovan's Gun*, p. 83). More comprehensively, the hero of another work thinks this way, in a moment of doubt: "True, Maule surrounded himself with hardcases, but all strong men through history had done the same. He had corrupted the law, but even in politics what strong man hadn't?" (*The Deserters*, p. 43).

Men in Short who are bent on revenge are often portrayed as pushed by a fate which they cannot defy. Thus, when Dave Nash's man is beaten to death by Virg Lea (among others), Dave simply must saddle up and go kill Virg. We read that Dave "had no taste for this chore. But it was one that had to be done, and that custom had put upon him, just as it had allowed him to tell [Sheriff] Crew of his intentions. . ." (*Ramrod*, p. 118). Similarly, when Carrie Bentall objects to Will Gannon's assumption of the obligation to obtain revenge, their conversation reveals his sense of fatality: " 'What do you want me to do, Carrie?' " Her answer indicates Short's sense of her imperfect acceptance of the fated Western code. " 'You asked me that before and I told you. I don't know. Keep on riding [away] . . .maybe.' " His rejection is immediate: " 'And leave. . .four murders unpunished?' " When she complains that he cannot succeed in his mission of revenge, his reply again suggests his sense of doom: "Maybe I can't. . ., but I don't run. . .' " (*The Whip*, pp. 89, 90) — indicating (by verb tense) that he operates in a kind of fated historical present. Other examples abound.[7]

Occasionally neither justice nor revenge is obtained in the end.

This nonclimax seems frustrating, somehow, given the formulaic nature of Short's production. But there it is, anyhow. Thus, in the tangled plot of *Ramrod*, villainous Connie Dickason warns Tom Peebles, who participated in her scheme of driving her own cattle over a cliff and blaming the enemy, " 'If I were you I'd ride as far away from here as a horse would take me' " (p. 178). He grins and vanishes; and Short lets him do so, even though the indirect results of Peebles's crime are several deaths, including that of a guiltless sheriff. Hugh Ganley of *Saddle by Starlight* is a villain who commits no vicious acts of violence personally; but since he does pay a pair of degenerates to do so for him, poetic justice is hardly served when Hugh simply pulls up stakes and leaves the region which he has helped to pollute. The worst villain to go scot free is Jimmy Oakes, who a dozen years earlier was seen by Dave Hardy knifing a bully to death in the silent moonlight; since Dave did not inform on him, Jimmy naturally agrees to " 'take. . .out' " Dave's enemy when drafted for the chore. " 'Tell me what I got to do' " (*Debt of Honor*, p. 116), Jimmy asks, as though he had no free will.[8]

We know that murderers often escape this way in real life, but it is shocking to read of such good fortune on their part in Short. At the end of *Donovan's Gun*, the whilom legalistic hero repeats to his patient beloved what he just told the criminal nesters: " 'I said everyone [*sic*] of them. . .could be charged with murder or arson, or both. I told them if they had the sense they were born with, they'd get out of the country before the marshal could move. . . . They didn't even talk it over. They just rode out' " (p. 165). Evil politicians also get off too easily sometimes. It is almost as though Short moralizes to the effect that if they do not actually do the trigger-pulling, their trigger men should take the fatal rap whereas the politicians will suffer enough if merely disgraced. Justin Rankin (*Debt of Honor*) and Governor Sam Kilmore, together with his party henchman Frank Jackson (*The Outrider*), are let off in this sadly typical American manner.

Short is also too kind to a few really vicious women in his novels. Thus dressmaker Bonnie Leal marries bigamistically— and with adultery in her heart—into the wealthy landholding Hethridge family early in *Donovan's Gun* and becomes a rich widow ten chapters later, never more to suffer economically. Anna Reeves, who is immoral throughout *Man from the Desert*, survives one lover's death, accepts a bribe of $30,000 to provide evidence which could hang another lover, and walks away from it all wealthy and still poisonously beautiful. She enunciates her philosophy of life early in the story: " 'I love money. I love survival. I love being loved by a rich man. The rest doesn't matter' " (p. 71).

IV *Loyalty, Duty*

" 'My orders were to retrieve or destroy them, sir. I'd like permission to carry them out' " (*Station West*, p. 108). Thus, Lieutenant Haven courteously (if ungrammatically) rebukes his commanding officer, when that worried man wants to call in the sheriff once Haven has located the stolen army uniforms. Short's best heroes want only the go-ahead from fate to carry out their wild missions.

Short fills his works with statements and dramatizations about one's doing his duty, being loyal to his boss, shepherding—if sometimes mercilessly leading—his men. Thus, when the hero of *The Branded Man* gets a job in an unpromising new land, we read that "Flood guessed he had been hired because he was a stranger, and because when a rancher hires a hand, he hires his unswerving loyalty and his life" (p. 40). Identically, Dave Nash, also a stranger newly employed in the region where *Ramrod* opens, reasons that "if you worked for a man you fought for him, too, no matter if you thought he was a fool and didn't believe in him" (p. 5).[9]

Sometimes a person tardily judges an associate to be loyal, and then that judgment proves fatal to the judge. For example, weak John Evarts of *Ride the Man Down* comes to see fierce, go-to-hell loyalty in Will Ballard, the ranch foreman he inherited when John's tough brother died. John and Will are going to oppose the encroachment of Bide Marriner, their land-greedy neighbor. "A change had come over John Evarts since yesterday, and he [Will] scarcely knew what to make of it himself. He knew what had done it. . .the second it took place. It was when he [John] had given his unspoken consent yesterday for Will to go ahead with the disarming of Bide and his men. . . . Up to that moment he [John] had been headed in one direction [toward capitulation]; at that moment, he swerved, and immediately Will Ballard was with him. It was that simple really" (p. 29). So John rides over to challenge another of Bide's men. But he encounters two of them and is immediately shot to death.

Two of the most fiercely demanding bosses in all of Short are
Phil Seay (*Hard Money*) and Will Gannon (*The Whip*). Seay
explains matters to his workers at the outset of his taking charge
of old Bonal's mine: "'I want loyalty,' Seay said vehemently.
'Bonal deserves it. I do. Any man worth his food deserves it!'" (p.
52).[10] Seay gives his men even more loyalty than he demands of
them: he once works unceasingly for three days and nights to
free some trapped miners, does so, and then collapses. Similarly,
Gannon as the new boss of the jeopardized stage line levels a curt
requirement at his dissolute friend and employee Hutch Forney:

> "The line pays you swing station people for two reasons—you're
> handy and you're reliable. When you get unreliable, we change."
> "You're talking about me?" Hutch asked.
> "I am. . . ." (p. 34)

Again as with Seay, Gannon gives his men as much protective
devotion as the loyalty he insists on from them. A minor stage
driver praises the hero in Carrie's presence: "'A man's going to
think twice before he stops my stage, points a gun at me, and tells
me to throw down the loot. He'll know he's got Gannon on his
neck and that Gannon won't quit till he gets him'" (p. 54). But
Carrie is an Easterner and remains unimpressed.

Not so one of the most observant of Short's heroines—Juliana
Frost of *Desert Crossing*. Criticizing deserter John Thornton for
being selfish, vain, stubborn, "'more than a little foolish,'" and
ignorant, she declines to accept hero Dave Harmon's rationaliza-
tion that they all saw Thornton under adverse conditions. She
replies, "'I saw him under the worst. So I know him. Dick
[Lieutenant Overman] didn't desert us. You didn't desert us.
That's the difference'" (p. 113). Oddly, when Kate Canady of
Donovan's Gun similarly praises Donovan, he responds in a
somewhat similarly defensive manner, to which she says,
"'You're not apologizing for your loyalty, are you?'" (p. 94).

Occasionally even Short's good women have divided loyalties
or go so far as to behave disloyally, through weakness or
ignorance. Thus, Tish Hammond keeps the hero Cole Halsey
dangling until quite late in *First Campaign*. Admittedly, her
father and his father are diametrically opposed politically, and,
admittedly, her father's newspaper-editor stooge has gossiped in

his columns against the entire Halsey family, Cole included. So it is not surprising, although it is sad, that the two young people bicker on and on, until Tish wearily says, " 'Go away, Cole. I'm not mad. I'm just. . .confused. . . . I'm tired of talking and I'm tired of thinking. My loyalties keep getting in the way of everything' " (p. 146). She even so treats a murderous villain as to lead him to believe that he may marry her a little later. Even worse is Nora Jenkins, who tells Johnny Hendry in *King Colt* not to see her again until he stops suspecting a friend of hers, who finally proves to be a consummate villain but who meanwhile dashingly hoodwinks her. Nora even focuses her amatory attention for a time on a nearby mine superintendent.[11]

Villains in Short are either loyal to their own men or so egocentric as to be loyal to nothing but their own evil purposes. Stupid gangs of villains in many of the novels hang together with an almost wistful fidelity. Examples include the rascals of *Marauders' Moon, Savage Range, Bought with a Gun, Hardcase, Ramrod, Fiddlefoot, Station West, Silver Rock, The Whip, The Some-Day Country, Paper Sheriff, The Guns of Hanging Lake, The Deserters,* and *The Outrider.* But once in a while Short dramatizes the villainy of a bad man in betraying, and even shooting, his own loyal subordinates. Thus when Sheriff Ed Linton (*Dead Freight for Piute*) notes that a certain thuggish crony suspects that he is being betrayed, the crooked lawman gets the bright idea of letting all his fellow villains kill each other off, which will leave the spoils for himself: "So Keen thought he was crossing him, selling him out. Linton hadn't thought of it before, but why not?" (p. 105). Why not, indeed?

Villainous Tate Riling of *Gunman's Chance* has an argument with one of his comrades in a wet, cold line shack, kills him by burying an axe in his chest, but then begins to worry: ". . .The mere fact that Sweet was killed would lose him these nesters that he needed now. Their loyalty right now was a pretty thin thing, and it would need only this to destroy it. On the other hand, he needed their loyalty and help for only two or three more days. . . . After that they could go to hell" (p. 150). At the end of *High Vermilion*, the two villains have a falling out, one is traitorous to the other by identifying certain incriminating evidence, and within seconds both are dead.

The most lurid example of disaffection occurs in *Donovan's Gun*, when hired killer Keefe Hart, savagely beaten up by his opponents but now mending, is trapped upstairs in a burning saloon (interestingly named the First Chance). He staggers to the window to observe a gunfight involving nesters and ranchers in the street below, and then we read:

Standing there, choking from the smoke billowing around him, eyes watering, he sought a target down on the street. Men were running, and he could not tell friend from enemy.

What's it matter? he thought savagely, and raised his gun to shoot at a man running.

That was when the enemy found him. He heard the first shot, but his own cry of anguish drowned the second shot, which killed him. (p. 126)

The most pusillanimous villain in all of Short is Les Seely of *The Man from Two Rivers.* Once he has the goods on a wanted criminal known as Will Musick, Seeley blackmails him to ambush two of Seely's own men and put the blame on the hero. Musick reluctantly does so, to save his own skin, but then thinks sourly: "He'd done the job he'd been paid for, but he didn't like any part of it. What kind of a son of a bitch would pay to have two of his own crew bushwhacked?" (p. 85).

V *Protect the Women*

Luke Short is in the tradition of Western fiction which portrays women as rare objects to be protected, soothed by courtesy, never offended, and encouraged to let their men think for them, urge them into homemaking and motherhood, and browbeat them if they hanker to reverse roles with men.

Men are men if they are strong and tough. And women are well advised to be meek and yielding and to recognize their limitations. If women want to occupy positions traditionally reserved for men, they should learn to shave. This is the highly conservative message which rings loud and deep through the length of Short's novels.

Now for some possibly offensive examples. The villainous Will Usher warns the hero of *Hardcase:* " 'I'm no woman, Dave. You move so much as a finger, and we'll blow you through that wall' " (p. 34). A rough customer in an aside insults one of the two hardcases in *Saddle by Starlight:* " 'That one on the right,' Bill Tench said softly. 'I'd like to take his hat off and see if he hasn't got long, brown pigtails' " (p. 26). In the next chapter, the insulted pair beat Tench to death. Obviously they would not wear pigtails.

On the other hand, pliant women win points with the men around them by being passive, helpless, and self-deprecating. Thus, when a minor young lady in *Dead Freight for Piute* applies for a job as bookkeeper for the outfit which she secretly blames for her brother's death, we read, "Letty Burns's gaze faltered and she bit her lip. Then she said sweetly, 'It's about a job. Oh, I know I'm a woman, but won't you listen to me?' " The sweet young thing will surely be hired after that. In fact, the hero puts it graciously: " 'There's no reason why a woman can't do as good book-work as a man, I reckon.' " Later, Letty continues to follow her successful strategy, when she begins to voice her fear for the safety of one of her handsome bosses: " 'Ted, I don't know how else to say it. You'll laugh at me and call me a woman. But I know I'm right' " (pp. 52, 114). She proves almost murderously capable and thus gives the lie to the general theory of the villain in *Man from the Desert*, in which we read: "Only now did anger come to Carrie. In his supreme arrogance, Ben had never consulted her. . . believing as he did that financial affairs were not a woman's business" (p. 51). Carol Lufton in *Gunman's Chance* makes her choice in men when she surrenders to villain Tate Riling and agrees to betray her father's legitimate interests. Tate browbeats her into adopting his view of things; then we read: "Carol hung her head a moment, so he couldn't see the tears that were making her eyes glisten. 'I've got to accept this,' she thought; a woman has always got to accept her man's truth, or he isn't her man" (pp. 49–50). Ironically, although she was his, he was never hers; and, anyway, her generalization is spurious rationalizing.

Just before the climactic chapter of *The Deserters*, loyal Laurie Mays, by now completely smitten by heroic Pete Brisbin, ineffectively warns him of danger; then, introducing some grotesquely chauvinistic dialogue, she adds hopelessly:

"I'll never understand you, never."

"Tomorrow you will" [Pete answers].

"What does that mean?"

"I can't tell you, Laurie. But it will answer a lot of questions you've asked me before. Trust me."

"But you don't trust me," Laurie said.

"I do," Peter said soberly. "I don't want you involved, is all."

"But involved in what?"
Pete shook his head. "Forget it, Laurie. . . ."
"You're treating me like a child," Laurie protested.
"Yes, like a very dear one. . . ." (p. 128)

A similar conversation occurs in *Donovan's Gun*, in which we find Kate Canady and Jim Donovan discussing the possibility of a range war. She remarks, " '. . .I don't think I'll sleep very well tonight after what you've told me.' " To this the hero counters easily, " 'Forget it. It's man's stuff. It won't touch you. Now good night, Kate' " (p. 68).[12]

One of the most moving passages in all of Short comes in *First Claim*, when the villain Tucker Weybright's mistress Hannah, who is mistreated and even has their little daughter to care for, finally shuts her door on Tucker with these bitter words: " 'We're through, Tucker! . . . Tomorrow I'm leaving.' " He replies with a superior jeer, " 'For where?' " to which she proudly explains, " 'I heard Kelsey [her saloon-keeper boss] tells you there were only four women in here today. One of them was my married sister. She's the one who told me what these people thought of you and what you were trying to do to Ballew. I'm moving in with her' " (p. 125). Out of context, this passage is less moving than it is for readers who have seen how Hannah has been enslaved by Tucker's sensuality, has been treated courteously by Ballew, and must all this time have regarded her married sister as a shining example of success, a role model, in the woman-oppressing West.

Now for one of the funniest passages in all of Short pertaining to women and their rights. It occurs in *Desert Crossing*. A military man, an army veteran, an Eastern civilian, and the heroine have been discussing the use of military titles, first names, and the like in polite conversation. The heroine addresses the hero now: " 'Are you of Dick's school, Mister Harmon?' At Dave's nod, she said, 'Then it's Dick [Lieutenant Overman], Dave [formerly Captain Harmon], and John [Thornton, Eastern villain]. That should make me Juliana [Frost] to all of you.' " Now comes the wild line: " '*Miss* Juliana,' Overman corrected her. 'Women have to be addressed by rank so we men know who we're free to kiss or to propose to.' " And the reactions? "Juliana chuckled, but there was a frown on Thornton's face. Lieutenant Overman's harmless whimsy and gallantry apparently did not amuse him, Dave noted" (p. 30). The assumptions here are all conservative: Juliana not only is victimized by but also has adopted the wrong-headed notions of her "society"; Thornton frowns only because he wants Juliana for himself and evidently sees Overman as a threat to that desire; and Dave characterizes Overman's sexist remarks as merely whimsical and gallant (and so, perhaps, does Short).

Like Miss Juliana, Sophie Barrick in *The Guns of Hanging Lake* preserves her image of agreeable innocence. She declines the hero's offer of a little pick-me-up whiskey in a hotel lobby by means of this demure generalization: " '. . .A woman doesn't drink in public' " (p. 34). Also like Juliana, Belle Cope in *The Outrider* readily acknowledges the superior strength and stamina of men, once she volunteers to go by train to Twin Buttes and nurse the hero, Will Christie, back to health after his near-fatal beating. We read that "the next morning, not very early, Belle went to the hotel room desk" to ask that breakfast be sent up to Will. She learns that the stoical fellow has already eaten and is on his feet: "He was dressed in clean range clothes, and except for his battered face and the bandages he looked as fit as ever" (p. 108). She asks if another day in bed would help, but he must be off and after the criminals.

In *Debt of Honor* Reeves Cable must explain to his foster mother Cornelia's lovely but seemingly naive Eastern niece Beth how to mix drinks. " 'Does she know how?' " Reeves first asks, soberly, noting her delightful freckles and silently thinking that "if she ever tried to hide them, he would spank her."[13] When she says, " 'Why, you just pour whiskey in a glass, don't you?' " he counters humorously, " 'Only if you've just come off roundup. Other times, when you've got ice, you pour a half a glass of water over it. Then you pour from the bottle until you get the color you want.' " Instead of taking offense, Beth asks what color he wants, is told " 'as brown as you can get it,' " and then—we read—"Beth poured a very dark drink for Reeves and a very light one for Cornelia and herself" (p. 107).

As we can readily see, in Short's novels the man leads, informs, and instructs, while the good woman serves and waits. If she domineers or demeans her man, he will eventually drop her, and all the sooner if her ethics in the double-standard world of the West are lower than or simply as low as his. Thus, when Frank Chess, the soiled titular hero of *Fiddlefoot*, decides to confess his

criminal past to Carrie Tavister, the judge's daughter, the most
he feels he can hope for is for her to rebuke him loftily and then
maybe forgive him. Confessing is going to be almost impossible,
Frank fears, because—as he earlier opines—' ". . .I did a shady
job for Rhino, a job that would lose me Carrie if she ever found it
out. . . . She's the only kind and decent person I've known and
I've treated her badly. I'll do anything—*anything* to keep from
losing her.' " "Anything" finally includes admitting to Carrie that
he wore a stolen army uniform to swindle ranchers out of good
horses. Imagine his surprise when she answers, " 'Who knows it?
You were never challenged, were you?' " Realizing that "*She
hasn't forgiven me because she doesn't even know I've done
wrong*" (pp. 127-28, 132), Frank breaks their years-long
engagement and walks out of her life.[14]

One way men treat women properly in Short is not to avoid
fighting so much as simply to avoid doing so in front of them.
More than a dozen shootouts and allied fatalities in Short are
delayed because women are present at an otherwise opportune
time for a fight. Here are some examples. The worried villain in
Saddle by Starlight agrees to meet with the hero only if the
heroine is present:

> A sudden contempt came into Julia's eyes. "Are you afraid to go
> alone?"
> "You're damn right I am" Ganley said flatly. "It's too easy to shoot a
> man and dump him down a handy mine shaft. . . ." (p. 100)

The clear implication is that villain and woman would never be
bushwhacked and then dumped together. In *Play a Lone Hand*,
vinegary old Mrs. Grady Sebree orders the hero to put up his
gun: " 'I forbid you. . . . There is no gunfire allowed at Torreon
[her evil husband's ranch]' " (p. 72). Jen Truro feels safe while
she is riding to wounded Reese Branham's rescue in *Paper
Sheriff*, even though the villain is still shooting: " 'He isn't going
to shoot me. He's already had the chance' " (p. 116), she
reassures her wounded lover. Amusingly, if a woman stumbles
onto a fight in progress, the combatants sometimes pause to
order her away out of sight again. For an imperfect example, we
have the following early in *Silver Rock:*

> But Hodes was down flat on his back, arms wrapped around his belly,
> knees almost touching his chin. He was gagging for air with an ugly

sobbing noise. Tully walked over to him and was only then aware of
Sarah Moffit standing against the closed corridor door. Tully said
harshly, "Get back in there, you fool!"

A startled look came into Sarah's eyes and she obeyed swiftly, and
now Tully put his attention to Hodes. . . . (pp. 28-29)

A stronger, more personally daring, and hence less commendable woman might have walked on in and stopped the mayhem.
Holly Heath of *Rimrock* is such a woman and does break up what
might have become an ugly fight between Dave Borthen and
Chief Buford. But such unladylike masculinity in Holly is partly
what earns her the heroine's offensively stated rebuke late in the
novel: " 'Mrs. Heath,' she said, 'you want to be a man so damn
badly, have you ever thought of shaving twice a day?' " (p. 126).
The sheriff in *The Primrose Try* uses similar language while
commending the heroine's aid in the cause of justice: " 'Well,
Tenney, you've earned a deputy's badge over these last few days.
Still, I don't think a person should wear one who's never shaved,
do you?' " The resourceful young woman's response? "Tenney
laughed. . ." (p. 64).

VI *Other Important Themes*

Three other valuable messages also ring through Short's
fiction. They are: bury the dead, improve if you see that you
should, and do not seek joy directly.

In more than a dozen novels Short dramatizes the hold which
the past has on his central characters. Thus the hero of *The
Branded Man* undertakes a mission which comprises the whole
novel, not knowing whether his dead brother was guilty of
rustling or not, but knowing that he himself must come to terms
with the past in order to go on thereafter. Central figures in *The
Man on the Blue, Bold Rider, Bought with a Gun, Gunman's
Chance, Hardcase, Fiddlefoot, Play a Lone Hand,* and to some
extent *Silver Rock* all have uneasy pasts to live down; and they
do so by seizing second chances and making something noble
with them. *High Vermilion* develops this theme especially well,
since it has an epiphanic moment during which the hero stops
running from his past and turns over a new leaf.

In a few novels, the past, festering because it is unforgotten
but not useful, is symbolized by a dead woman, either the hero's
wife or his fiancée. Embarking on new adventures, either for

revenge or in an effort to forget, the hero proceeds through a stage of guilt to one of laying the past to rest—and then turns to new love and the future. Following this pattern are *Ramrod*, *Coroner Creek*, *The Whip*, *The Primrose Try*, and *The Deserters*. In *Coroner Creek* this figurative burial of the dead is expressed in a moving if somewhat brutal way. When the dead fiancée's murderer finally lies dead before him, Chris Danning says to himself, " *'I'm rid of you now, Bess. At last I'm rid of you."* A page later, facing his new love, he says, " 'She's gone, she's buried, and I'm done with it. I'm—' " (pp. 149, 150). What follows is intensely moving.[15]

Two other novels—*Desert Crossing* and *Paper Sheriff*—handle the past with special effectiveness. In *Desert Crossing* the hero's now dead army past is symbolized by his eye patch, the consequence of a wound which caused him to muster out. He cannot come to terms with that military past and thinks himself freakish in appearance until the heroine tells him that she wants more than fun from a man and regards his patch as a badge of honor.[16] In *Paper Sheriff*, we have a switch: Reese Branham tries to bury his past love for Jen Truro, since Callie, albeit a rustler from a homicidal clan, is his wife. But at novel's end, Callie is gunned down—by something like a *deus ex machina*, it would seem to most readers—and Reese is free to turn back the clock with wonderful Jen.

Short's heroes regularly trust themselves, and their loyal sidekicks, too; but it takes many of those heroes a long while to understand themselves, to initiate efficacious self-reform. Three examples will suffice. Owen Daybright (*Vengeance Valley*) is so anxious to be generous to those who have befriended him that he is blind to his own best interests until it is almost too late. Jim Donovan (*Donovan's Gun*) wrongly fancies that he can remain aloof from the range war crackling all about him; the novel brilliantly stages the steps of his dawning self-awareness. And Tully Gibbs (*Silver Rock*) agonizes through nine-tenths of his story until he can no longer live with himself but must confess the baseness of his motivation; then, rather too suddenly, all's well.

Virtually every Short novel demonstrates that peripheral hedonistic vision is best. Look directly for happiness, and it will elude you. Seek something harsh, be stoical, aid others—and at the end of your trail will be bliss. This is what happens to hero after hero: a man, against his will, is put into the custody of a gnarled old rancher and winds up marrying his daughter (*Marauders' Moon*); a man seeks the killer of a rich prospector and falls in love with that victim's incognito heiress (*Bounty Guns*); a man takes a freight job with a supposed uncle and marries the sister of that fraud's competitor (*Dead Freight for Piute*); and a man seeks revenge upon his half-brother, succeeds, and saves the villain's widow for himself (*Trouble Country*). The point of the pattern, which is ingeniously varied, is obvious.

VII   *Minor Themes*

Three minor themes remain for elucidation. They are woven into the music of Short's novels like noisy little melodies and are: West versus East, ends justify means, and mobs fail.

Like Zane Grey in many of his novels, Short often has women with a veneer of Eastern respectability enter or return to the West and find out—often harshly—what life is really all about. This is the case with Sylvia Waranrode (*Brand of Empire*), Celia Wallace (*Dead Freight for Piute*), Elizabeth Lowell (*And the Wind Blows Free*), Carrie Bentall (*The Whip*), Julia Frost (*Desert Crossing*), Beth Fanning (*Debt of Honor*), Sarah Hethridge (*Donovan's Gun*), and Belle Cope (*The Outrider*). Short most obviously satirizes the East by pointing out the dry-as-dust academic nature of the Eastern experiences of Elizabeth Lowell, who is "distantly related to the Boston Lowells" (p. 2) and who likes the poetry of Henry Wadsworth Longfellow, and Beth Fanning, who while still back home " 'got a job doing research for a professor who was writing a history of New England' " (p. 20).

Short never overlooks an opportunity to have his characters fashion generalizations favorable to the West and derogatory to the East, by contrast. Thus we have the following: " 'You see, in the East, when a man like Waranrode is accused of this crime, he hires the best lawyers in the country. Here [in the West] a man sees to it that he isn't accused' " (*Brand of Empire*, p. 167). " 'My friend, out here in the West it doesn't seem to be the custom to read things you sign. You trust a man. But I came from the East, where lawyers are a little sharper than these homespun orators of yours' " (*Savage Range*, p. 151; the speaker is a criminal). "As for the ethics of it [Mary Kincheon thinks], weren't Big Men stealing lands all over the West, sometimes with the collusion of the [federal, i.e., Eastern-establishment] Land Office itself?" (*Play a Lone Hand*, p. 135). And "During Indian troubles [Silence Frane thinks], the Army was always too late to avert disaster and usually too inept to catch and punish. It attracted the dregs of the Eastern cities and its officer corps was made up of men who had failed in civilian life" (*The Some-Day Country*, p. 44).

The most chilling demonstration of the questionable thesis that a good end justifies callous means comes in *Raiders of the Rimrock*, in an early chapter of which the hero, Tim Enever, suggests to Martha Kincaid that to make the independent nesters aware that Warner Sands is their common enemy Tim might secretly shoot close to some of them and burn the barns of some others, and leave false clues pointing to Sands. Tim concludes, " 'You reckon they'd talk it over and decide to gang up for protection?' " The heroine's reaction is not exactly one of moral outrage. " 'I hoped you'd say that,' she said at last. 'Maybe you think I'm ruthless or cruel. I'm not. I don't always believe that the end justifies the means, but I do now' " (p. 20).

The entire matter of deliberate deception is important in Short. The hero in almost every one of his novels tells lies to survive. Pick any of the novels, and you will probably find at least eight or ten passages dotted with prevarications—many of them poetic and ingenious. Some of the most interesting samples are scattered through *The Guns of Hanging Lake*. In it, Traf Kinnard coaches the deputy sheriff in lies to tell suspected villains, rehearses a witness of murder in his false identity as Traf's girl friend's former boy friend's uncle, even persuades that frustrated would-be lover to lie in support of the falsehood, and fibs thus to a casual eavesdropper named Stapp: " 'Sure,' Traf said easily. Stapp sounded virtuous enough to be lying, he thought. Well, why not? He himself had just lied to Stapp" (p. 100). The hero of *The Stalkers*, who is in disguise much of the time, rehearses the heroine too: " 'Your story is this: you don't even know my name [false]; I didn't say where I was going [false]. And you're glad I'm gone [false] because I couldn't pay you or doc [true].' " The heroine is not offended but "laughed softly and said, 'I haven't lied since I was a little girl, but these lies I like' " (pp. 32–33).[17]

Sometimes if the villain lies the hero is offended.[18] But more often he is amused, since the truth, like a rifle or a chess man, is a legitimate weapon to be kept handy for the deadly games Short's matched adversaries play. Other weapons are legitimate as well. Both good and evil characters in Short use theft, forgery, arson, cattle stampeding, kidnapping, and deliberately fatal and near-fatal gunfire as means to attain desired ends. If you fight, fight to win; it is irrelevant to pass judgment on the means used.[19]

The Old West was an arena of individual effort, reward, and loss. Not surprisingly, therefore, fiction about it extols the virtues of individual effort. One efficient way of dramatizing feisty independence is to pit the lonely hero against a mob, which then loses. In Short, mob action is almost always ineffective. Shamrock Ireland (*The Man on the Blue*) outdistances the posse after him, turns back and watches it flounder, and later outfaces all such headless opponents. Similar posses figure in *Marauders' Moon, The Primrose Try,* and *The Man from Two Rivers.* Town leaders often get together in a body, and soldiers in the field move together; but usually neither group can thereafter match the resolution of the heroic individual. Perhaps Short has Will Ballard of the Hatchet ranch in *Ride the Man Down* unconsciously indulge in thematic symbolism of a profound nature when he gripes to old Joe Kneen, the sheriff, that no jury—ideally a rational body with a spokesman if not a leader— will vote to convict the blatant murderer of Will's boss: " 'This whole country's set to tear Hatchet apart [Will complains]. Try to get a jury that doesn't hate us. Try to get a jury that will try Cavanaugh [the murderer] and not Hatchet. Can you promise to get one, Joe?' " (p. 75). Three chapters later, Will, having self-reliantly convicted and sentenced Cavanaugh in his own mind, appoints himself firing squad—with Joe at his side.

CHAPTER 7

Short's Artistry (1)

S O far, we have been considering mainly the *what* of Luke
Short's novels. Now it is time for us to consider aspects of his
artistry—the *how* of his works.

The word "authentic" is used the most often to describe
Short's fiction. But in addition, high praise can be given to his
roaring-fast openings, his handling of point of view, his functional
dialogue, the clever ways in which he characterizes, and his
sense of humor, as well as his verisimilitude. And much else.

I *Openings*

Without exception, Short begins his novels *in medias res*, and
almost always effectively. To be sure, *The Feud at Single Shot,
Marauders' Moon,* and *King Colt* start uncertainly; but they are
early works, written in the mid-1930s, before the author had
found his formula and true voice. The whole first chapter, staged
aboard a moving train, of *The Feud at Single Shot* is confusing,
with major and minor characters introduced by action, trait, and
feature rather than name or hint as to their position on any moral
scale. Further, the hero is passive when compared to a certain
resourceful redheaded man. However, the poker game in
progress is an apt metaphor for much of the ensuing plot—
indeed, for much action later in Short's canon and in Western
fiction generally. *Marauders' Moon* opens in a bewildering
fashion, with the omniscient narrator zooming down on Iron Hat
Petty, a character who later has no function; further, the fellow
does not trouble even to watch as a sequence of five unnamed,
undifferentiated men is described—poised for nefarious action.
Chapter 1 of *King Colt* is technically Short's worst opening. In it,
a prospector named Picket-Stake Hendry is discovered musing
on a victim he has just killed. He recalls events of two days

earlier which led to his gunning down the evil man; he then
thinks that he himself might have been killed and nobody but his
irresponsible foster-son Johnny Hendry would have cared. This
leads to his semiflashback reminiscence about Johnny and then a
grotesque decision to dress the fortuitously faceless corpse in
Picket-Stake's clothes so that Johnny will think he is dead, and
will then mature and reform. Picket-Stake then disappears from
the novel until Chapters 10, 18, and 24 (the last).

On the other hand, Short's other novels open skillfully. These
openings function in one of four main ways: to characterize the
hero, to introduce his main motive, to present symbolic action, or
to throw the reader into a tangled plot.

The hero is often quickly and definitively presented at the
outset, for example, in *War on the Cimarron* and *Station West*.
He may be initially depicted as mean, with the clear hint that he
will mend in the course of the action, as in *The Man on the Blue*,
Bounty Guns, and *Play a Lone Hand;* or naively neutral, hence
soon to be disillusioned and rendered active, as in such works as
Vengeance Valley and *Donovan's Gun*.

Often the opening action exposes what will be the hero's main
motive. Thus, one hero rides into a cattleman-sheepman
controversy to clean it up *(Raiders of the Rimrock);* another tries
to unite his cattle-raising neighbors against nesters but cannot
(Saddle by Starlight); still another quits his salesman's job to seek
uranium *(Rimrock);* and yet another gets his orders to find an
army deserter-murderer *(The Deserters)*.

Occasionally, to hint at what will become the hero's motive,
Short stages symbolic action in his openings. Here are the best
examples. In *Raw Land* we first meet the hoodwinked hero as he
is rendezvousing with his faithful, hypocritical "friend" in the
dark, outside town. The hero of *Dead Freight for Piute* is first
seen riding in a stage coach with the scared heroine, who after
she is robbed by unknown thugs is rescued by the hero, of whom,
however, she remains suspicious; he later joins her freighting
operation, participates in more rescues, but long remains under
that cloud of suspicion. Jim Garry in *Gunman's Chance* is cold
and alone, when suddenly a stampede of strange cattle destroys
his meager possessions—symbolic perhaps of the inessential
remnants of his now self-despised past. Then a man comes along
and offers Jim his chance. In *Ambush*, the hero is at first of two
minds concerning scout-work for the army, since he admires the

Apaches; he remains uncertain throughout most of the ensuing action. The two principals of *The Man from Two Rivers* meet during a storm seemingly generated to force them into partnership and back to his home again, instead of farther down the river in an abortive escape from his—their—reality, their destiny.

Most often, Short simply opens a novel by reaching out, grabbing the reader, and thrusting him into the midst of ongoing action. Almost before he knows it, the reader has met half a dozen or so important characters and is swirling on the tide of a rushing plot. Thus, in the short first chapter of *Sunset Graze*, the hero is met on a dusty road (itself both a symbolic and a foreshadowing element), hails a stagecoach, enters it, sits on the heroine's hat, enters the town of his future troubles, beats up one villain and begins to question another, confers with the sluggish sheriff about his mission, hints that he will resist efforts to hustle him on out of town, and learns that a woman important to his investigation has disappeared. All this in the first eleven pages.

Openings in Short sometimes function in less categorizable manners. *Hard Money* begins with a description of a town which is less important than the mining region outside it; *Desert Crossing*, at a seaport which the ensuing action almost immediately leaves behind. *The Primrose Try, The Guns of Hanging Lake,* and *Three for the Money* open with objective, almost reportorial accounts of murder; in none is the hero anywhere near yet, but the reader is willing to hurry on, meet him, and anticipate justice or revenge. *First Claim* begins with taut symbolic action: we are invited to look over a hostler's shoulder at two people. One is old Lynch Weybright, who is bulling his way through the horse traffic in town, slugs a horse which is in his way, and trudges on. The other is young Giff Ballew, who is riding his horse on the wrong side of the street, and hence traffic pulls away from him. The rest of the novel depicts the collision course of these two antagonists, as one moves with but tries to stop the flow of events, while the other— certainly "on the wrong side" (p. 2) of the entire community at first—reaches and claims his destiny, which is his dead father's land. The first three paragraphs are a microcosm of all essential subsequent action. One novel, *The Stalkers*, starts as the heroine, after the funeral of her remaining parent, is being comforted by the local physician, whose latest patient is the amnesiac hero. We meet, in this order, heroine, doctor, and hero; not until the end does the heroine pair off with the doctor rather than with the hero. In the first chapter, the ordering of introductions is a bit of foreshadowing.

II *Point of View*

Short rarely troubled his mind with the modern technical problem of point of view. With the one exception of *And the Wind Blows Free*, which has a first-person-singular narrator, Short employs the no-nonsense omniscient narrator who in each novel mainly follows the activities of the hero, releases information so as to create the greatest possible suspense, but once in a while withholds facts and motivations awkwardly. Never is Short's storyteller even slightly literary in a way to draw attention to himself and away from the events being reported; never does he adopt a supercilious, satirical, ironic, or folksy tone; always he aims at a utilitarian, lean prose style.[1] If he is lyrical or humorous or cynical, it is always because the situation is evocative; such notes are sounded quickly, and then the narrator picks up his yarn again. Short is an action novelist, not a historian, philosopher, or poet.

It takes the reader almost no time to discover who the protagonist of a given Short novel is. In all but two cases, he is focused on sympathetically in the first chapter. Only in *King Colt* and *The Some-Day Country* (two of Short's least effective works) do we first meet the heroes in Chapter 2. In about a dozen novels, the hero appears after a touch or two of introductory staging without him. For example, *Three for the Money* first has the robbery-killing; and then Cam Holgate appears, reports that he will earn the reward money, and begins his detective work. In three instances *(Brand of Empire, Summer of the Smoke,* and *The Stalkers)*, the hero appears late in the first chapter, injured and hence out of the initial action. In all other cases, the main character puts in a prompt appearance. The first sentence of *War on the Cimarron* names the hero; the second sentence of *The Branded Man* does; the third in *Coroner Creek;* and so on.

One of Short's most effective point-of-view devices is what we may call cinematic. Short will follow a main character to a new locale, observe and listen in, and then let him go out again while the sound camera, so to speak, remains at the same locale. For example, at the end of Chapter 2 in *Play a Lone Hand*, Giff Dixon shadows a suspicious puncher from the newspaper office up the street, into the hotel, up the stairs, and after him into the villain Grady Sebree's room. There, another of Giff's enemies is lying in bed recovering from a beating. Gun in hand now, Giff alerts all who are present—including two strange cowboys—to his animosity, then backs out, and closes the door. We then read:

> As soon as the door was closed, both punchers lunged out of their chairs, headed for it.
> "No!" Sebree said sharply. The two halted, and looked sullenly at him. "Go downstairs and wait, all of you."
> The three went out, and Sebree made a slow circle of the room, head lowered on his chest. (p. 53)

The indication of focus, motion, and talk are all like elements in a movie scenario.[2]

Occasionally, when the hero is asleep or knocked cold, all action stops. Thus, Giff Ballew early in *First Claim* rightly calls a huge deputy clerk in the Harmony courthouse a liar but is then caught off guard and instantly slugged unconscious. The action is suspended until he recovers. We follow so closely on the heels of Short's heroes that when one is decked, we expect the action to stop until he comes to again. Thus, when Will Gannon of *The Whip* crawls and lurches, horribly shotgunned in the back and side, to temporary safety, our point of view remains strictly within his wavering awareness. At one point we read:

> . . .he leaned against the logs of the store, waiting for the fresh pain to subside a little, closing his eyes against the drench of perspiration that was his body's protest against the pain.
> When he opened his eyes, he saw several horsemen gathering around the lantern by the feed barn. . . . (p. 71)

Since Short's stories all concern specific heroic action, it comes as a surprise to read, as once in a while we do, that a hero has been rapped into unconsciousness but that talk continues over his inert form. Yet this is what occurs a few times, with notable awkwardness in *Raw Land* (pp. 44-45) and *Three for the Money* (pp. 27-29).

One of the most remarkable uses of the restricted point of

view in all of Short occurs in *The Whip*, when wounded Gannon, whom Carrie has now undressed, bathed, and put face down into her bed to hide, comes to again after six days and nights of delirium:

> The first thing Will was conscious of was that it was night. The second was the scent of a woman's hair that seemed to come from the bedding in which his face was buried. The third thing he became aware of was that his body was as drenched with wetness as if he had just been pulled from water.
>
> Turning his head, he studied the small square of window through which he could hear the soft rustle of wind on grass.
>
> He had no notion of where he was, and when he tried to push himself to his elbows and look about the room the knifing pain slashed across his back and he subsided. Slowly, painstakingly, he tried to piece memory together. He remembered the ambush in the corral and his escape to the prairie. But how had he arrived here? (p. 81)

The sequence of sensations and thoughts is accurate: first a sense of darkness, then smell, then feeling, and then motion and specific sight, next an effort at more movement, then pain, and finally an attempt at recollection and thought.

When it suits his narrative purpose, Short moves from one scene to another one, the second often distant from the first (usually in space, more rarely in time), rather like Thackeray, Hugo, or Tolstoy; again, Short does so without troubling his head about post-Jamesian niceties. For the best example, we may look at *Desert Crossing*, which easily moves from Harmon's wagon train to Lieutenant Miller's camp to the villains' hideout to the desert which two soldiers, then one, try to cross. When Short "violates" the modern restricted point of view in lesser ways, he always has a legitimate technical reason for doing so; and always the reader rushes on, anxious to get back to the hero as quickly as possible.[3]

Short uses the stream-of-consciousness technique in a tentative, timorous manner. As he employs it, this device may be characterized as a kind of dialogue between character and reader. Short has a person, usually the hero but occasionally another, say something to himself—in italics. We recall that at the end of *Coroner Creek* the hero addresses the spirit of his dead fiancée: " *'I'm rid of you now, Bess'* " (p. 149). Similarly, just before Giff Dixon of *Play a Lone Hand* follows the puncher to the hotel, he wonders about the suspicious fellow: *"I've seen him*, he thought, *and where?* but he couldn't place him. Then it came to him. *The fellow who. . ."* (p. 52). While Carrie hides her hero in *The Whip*, she silently hopes that the prowling villains will leave the premises pronto: "Under her she felt rather than heard Gannon stir [at this time he is hidden on the floor beneath her bed] and silently she prayed, *Let them get out of here, now!"* (p. 81).

III *Dialogue*

If Short is often not subtle in manipulating point of view, he is starkly brilliant in handling dialogue. His characters listen attentively to each other. Their talk is for the purpose of revealing important information to the reader, concerning people and their actions. Short's characters speak differently one from another. As is to be expected in Western fiction, talk in Short's works is normally clipped, terse, laconic, purposeful.[4]

Consider this hypnotic conversation in *First Campaign* between corrupt lawyer Abe Brandell, who has information for sale, and corrupt campaign-manager Bowie Sanson, who is willing to buy his candidate's victory. All non-dialogical prose, including attributions, are omitted; such words are meaningful enough, terse in themselves, but inessential here.

"Well?"

. . ."Want to get your candidate elected governor, Bowie?"

"Oh, no. . . . For a small sum, say a hundred dollars, you'll tell me how I can do it."

For a large sum, I'll show you."

"How large?"

"Fifteen thousand."

. . ."Good night, Abe. Close the door on your way out."

"You don't even want to hear how?"

"Not for that kind of money. No."

. . ."I brought three things with me tonight, Bowie. One is a gun. . . . The second is a bottle, from which I will now take a drink."

. . ."That document [the third item is an envelope] will defeat Governor Halsey and elect your boy Asa Forbes."

. . ."What's the gun for, Counselor?"

"To shoot you with if you don't return the document."

. . ."To be opened upon the death of Governor Harold Halsey

[Bowie reads the writing on the envelope]. . . . A little premature, aren't you, Abe?"
"That's beside the point. Read it."
"This is privileged, isn't it?"
"Also beside the point."
. . ."Who was it said, 'In God we trust, but lawyers never'? . . . [Bowie reads the contents of the envelope.] It's notarized, I see."
"I was a lawyer once. Remember?
. . ."When do you want your fifteen thousand, Counselor?" (pp. 2–3)

Sometimes very little conversation is followed by a maximum of action. By way of preface to the following example, let me report that Dave Nash, hero of *Ramrod*, has been drinking in the strange town of Signal, following the death of his wife and then that of his young son; that Frank Ivey has just run Dave's cowardly new boss Walt Shipley out of town; and that Red Cates, an Ivy man, thinks it might be fun to razz Dave. The scene is a saloon.

Dave. . .was almost alongside Frank Ivey when Red Cates, next to Ivey, half came around and drawled, "Hear your boss lit a shuck [i.e., ran off]." . . .
"Did he?" Dave asked.
. . ."You'll have to get a new sucker to pay for your drinks now, booze-head."
Dave regarded him mildly, said quietly, "I'd go careful, Red."
Red glanced over at Ivey and grinned. "Sounds like Shipley, don't he?"
"No," Dave said gently. "He just talked."
"So do you."
Dave hit him.

After the fight, which ends with Red unconscious and with a broken nose, Dave and Ivey stare at each other, then speak.

Frank said, "A man would never do that to me."
"Or me," Dave said. (pp. 27–28)

Most women in Short speak infrequently, and then usually to men. Rarely are a couple of women involved in dialogue with a man at the same time. But a dramatic exception occurs in *Saddle by Starlight,* when cruel Anse Heth argues with his kind wife

Eleanor in their kitchen because she sent her helper Julia Rainey
to warn the hero of danger. Cast in drama form, the dialogue (all
verbatim from the novel) would go something like this:

[Eleanor:] I sent her.
[Heth:] You sent her? . . . Then you can send her back again, send
her clear away from here for good.
[Eleanor:] No, Anson.
[Heth:] I say, get her out of here in an hour!
[Eleanor, rising from her chair:] I told you before, . . . if Julia goes,
I go.
[Heth, shoving her back down:] No, you don't. . . . You're not going
off this place, and I'm telling the crew that.
[Eleanor, standing again:] You can't keep me here! I won't—
[Heth, clouting her back down, then leaning on the table:] You're
not going anywhere, lady! . . . Suppose you stay home and be a wife
for a change. [To Julia] Get out! [Heth leaves the room.]
[Julia:] Believe me, it's best that I go.
[Eleanor:] Go where?
[Julia:] It doesn't matter, just so it's away from here. Please don't ask
me to stay. It's not fair to you.
[Eleanor:] I can't insist, Julia. Next time he'd hit you. [Julia goes to
her room to pack. Eleanor follows.] I've thought of something. (pp.
78–80)

The most apt and summary speech by any Short protagonist
comes at the end of *Man from the Desert*, when in three brief
sentences the hero reminds the heroine that he volunteered to
help her because he was indebted to her uncle, that the danger is
over now, and that the reward of her love makes it all
worthwhile. He says, " 'Trouble I asked for. Trouble I owed.
Trouble I'm glad I had' " (p. 170).
One unusual form of dialogue which Short uses, though
sparingly, and which I have rarely seen any other novelist use is
this: a speaker makes a statement or asks a question, then
continues to speak; thereafter, the person to whom he has been
talking responds to the initial statement or question, but ignores
the substance of the first speaker's later comment. For example:

"Does he deserve a dirty bushwhacking at the hands of Bonsell?" Jim
asked passionately. "He's paid his debt a thousand times over!"
"No," Cope answered. "He doesn't." (*Savage Range*, p. 107)

Or this:

> "Can I be the judge of that, Con? Why am I killing him?"
> Con and Harrington looked at each other, and Sam thought, *Here it is.*
> Seeley Carnes spoke for the first time. "No." (*The Primrose Try*, p. 50)

Another dialogical device which Short uses and which aids in the creation of verisimilitude is the later misquoting of an earlier comment—unintentional but credible because of the quoter's inevitably faulty memory. For one example among a dozen or more, Beth in *Debt of Honor* is thinking to herself, "What was it he [Reeves Cable] had said about the Mortensens? 'If they ever did an honest thing, it was only by accident.'" But what Reeves really said was this: "'Beth, we're dealing with a whore and a man who took a bribe. If either of them has ever done an honest thing in their lives, it was by accident'" (pp. 69–70, 68).

IV *Characterization*

E. M. Forster has usefully divided fictional characters into flat ones and round ones. Flat characters, he explains, "are constructed round a single idea or quality." On the other hand, round ones have, in the words of a later helpful critic, "some complexity, a credible consistency, and either some normality in relation to the society in which they move, or some explanation of the deviance."[5] Since Forster adds that "Dickens' people are nearly all flat," it is surely no insult to contend at the outset that most of Short's are, too. Forster says that flat characters are "easily recognized whenever they come in."[6] All but a few of Short's are thus recognizable; those few are hypocrites who fool the protagonists for a time (for example, Senator Maitland of *Hardcase*), disguised helper figures (for example, Perry MacElvey of *Coroner Creek*), or red herrings (for example, Bill Geary of *Last Hunt*). Even they are flat in their own way.

Short characterizes with broad strokes. He sketches the hero's physical appearance quickly: hair, eyes, eyebrows, nose, jaw, bulk of chest, hands, length of leg, gait, ability with a horse, dexterity with guns. Short usually gives his heroes pleasant, simple first names and neutral Anglo-Saxon last names. Thus, we have several heroes named Dave, Jim, Sam, and Will, and two or three named Cole, Frank, Giff, John, Pete, and Tim. These ten first names account for well over half of Short's heroes. Most of the other heroes have common enough first names as well, such as Chris, Hal, Lee, Mark, and Phil. The remaining heroes sometimes have either surnames for first names (Cameron, Hobart, Larkin, and the like) or onomastically symbolic ones (Poco, Shamrock, Winfield). Only with his fifteenth novel did Short repeat a hero's first name (see *War on the Cimarron* and *Barren Land Showdown*). Heroes' last names are naturally more varied; but once again, they are usually common enough ones, familiar to Anglo-European readers, for example, Christian, Cousins, Flood, Holgate, Kinsman, Nash, and Turner. A pair of unrelated heroes are named Jim Wade (see *Savage Range* and *And the Wind Blows Free*). Another pair share the same last name of Danning (*Raw Land* and *Coroner Creek*) for no apparent reason.

The villains are also quickly described as to their physical appearance. They are usually shorter than their heroic nemeses; that similarity in villains aside, however, they then usually divide into broad, massive hulks and older, fatter, sloppier mounds of evil. Villains' names are ingenious and revealing, and there are more villains in Short than heroes to challenge the novelist's name-calling propensities. Curiously, he has many villainous Bens; in addition, we find several Hughs, and a few Arnies (two of them knife-toting Finns), Reds (hardly a name), and Wills, and a pair each of Albies, Franks, Jesses, Santees, Sauls, Tates, and Will-Johns. Odd first names of villains include Bowie, Bide, Espey, Jud,[7] Loosh, Otie, Servel, Wake, and Younger (from the nefarious gunslinging Younger brothers, undoubtedly). Villains' last names in Short often include harsh "k" sounds, as in Carmody, Cates, Cleff, Coombs, Corb, Courteen, Cruver, Kilgore, Fasken, Feldhake, and Westock. Terse, odd names include Fitz, Gore, Gove, Hoad, Hodes, Taff, and Traff. Two villains in unrelated works are named Chance (*Sunset Graze* and *Three for the Money*). Two villains in back-to-back novels have the same first name, Tate (*Gunman's Chance* and *Hardcase*).

Short names his heroines with a bit more versatility and memorableness. He offers us several Kates, a few Beths, Carries (one ultimately not a sweet heroine), Celias, Marys, and Marthas, a couple of Abbys, Amys, and splendid Jens. Surely the most tingling female names in all of Short are Jen Canafax (*Vengeance Valley*), Jen Truro (*Paper Sheriff*), and Tess Falette (*Fiddlefoot*). Short has the hero muse on Tenney Payne's unusual first name: "Strange name, and one Sam had never heard before, but oddly attractive" (*The Primrose Try*, p. 12; when they marry, she will become Tenney Kennery). The least attractive names of heroines are Ellen Preftake (*And the Wind Blows Free*), Sarah Morfitt (*Silver Rock*), and Stacey Wheelis (*The Man from Two Rivers*).

As for these female characters' physical appearance, Short quickly describes their hair, eyebrows, eyes, noses, smiles, bosoms, heights, and manner of dressing. His three villainesses— Connie Dickason (*Ramrod*), Holly Heath (*Rimrock*), and Tina Bowers (*Three for the Money*)—are all enchantingly beautiful, and as deadly as glittering serpents.[8] Fallen angels, all, but with something of the celestial trailing from them still.[9]

Short is so unequivocally serious in his desire to write gripping Western action stories that he includes almost no comic-relief characters. So we have no fire-and-brimstone preachers,[10] no shotgun-riding old sidewinders, no talkative or taciturn barkeeps, no walrus-moustachioed barflies, no lachrymose swampers, no shrill mothers with mop and switches, no prissy schoolmarms, no heart-of-gold saloon floozies, and no extraneous brats of either sex.

The few exceptions approaching stereotypes include a fussy physician, too literate for his locale (Horace L. Benbow of *Brand of Empire*); a Bible-spouting harridan of a country wife (Mrs. Parker of *Donovan's Gun*); a genial, over-the-hill prostitute who on a bet parades down Main Street naked (Pearl of *The Stalkers*); and feisty old-timers who are almost funny (Ives of *Sunset Graze* and Asa Caskie of *The Guns of Hanging Lake*). The villain of *High Vermilion* drools tobacco juice so grotesquely that it is hard to take his machinations with total seriousness.

Short's West is a WASP hegemony. As such, it has little room, unfortunately, for blacks, Chinese, and Hispanic Americans, all of whom, without exception, are characterized by stereotyping. We have only one black cowboy. He is Curt, and we read of him mainly the following: "Pete kept his temper and replied that Martha Kincaid's Curt had seen them. Keith replied he didn't believe a damn nigger" (*Raiders of the Rimrock*, p. 56). Thereafter, Curt ceases to function in the action. Short's abbreviated gallery of blacks also includes a black barber *(The Feud at Single Shot);* some black troops, mentioned but not individualized *(And the Wind Blows Free);* black servants, both male and female *(And the Wind Blows Free, First Campaign);* maids in houses of prostitution *(Debt of Honor, The Stalkers);* ranch cooks *(Marauders' Moon, Guns of Hanging Lake);* and a steamboat steward *(The Man from Two Rivers).* Sadly typical of black speech in Short is the following, by a town black ordered to gallop with a message to a nearby fort: " 'Yassuh. I'se gone, boss' " *(Bold Rider,* p. 139).

Chinese in Short's American West are similarly stereotyped. In *The Branded Man, Raiders of the Rimrock, Bounty Guns,* and *Gunman's Chance,* they merely cook, grin, and chirp. For example, "At the Oriental Café, a cubbyhole of a place run by a Chinaman, Tip wolfed down his breakfast in silence. It seemed to him that the grinning Chinaman, with his affable gibberish, was the only friendly soul he had met in Hagen" *(Bounty Guns,* p. 24).

So also with Mexicans in Short. They are flat characters with only one exception, and function as farm hands, domestics, and mistresses. The only individualized Hispanic in all of Short is lovely, long-suffering, devout Rita Lopez Dana, the hero's sister-in-law in *Trouble Country,* Short's last novel. Even she is depicted partly as a sex object: "Rita halted in her tracks and turned. She was a short, slim, full-bosomed woman in her early thirties with dark hair and almost black eyes over a short, straight nose and full and generous mouth. . . . Rita moved ahead. . ., her taut haunches swinging enough to move the hem of her skirt from side to side" (pp. 72, 73).[11]

Instead of individualizing white minorities in the mines to any extent, Short seems to have found it easier to have his unpleasant characters mouth general racist remarks. We find such comments in abundance in *Hard Money, First Campaign, The Deserters,* and *The Outrider.* For example, one evil politician says to another in *The Outrider,* " 'All right. I feel sorry for those [dead and injured] miners, but nobody marched them into the Mary E [an accident-prone mine] at gunpoint. Everybody knows mines are dangerous, even the dumbest hunkie mucker. Still, they took the job' " (p. 21). This seems to be a sufficient reason for political resistance to more rigorous mine-safety laws. Incidentally, there are only two Jewish characters in Short. They are Mrs. Feldman, the music teacher in *Donovan's Gun*, and Marv Freeman, the store owner in *The Man from Two Rivers*. Both are minor figures.

We have almost sufficiently seen Short's treatment of American Indians. Never does the novelist get into the Indian consciousness. Late in his career, he did, to be sure, depict an Indian couple who display bravery, ingenuity, tolerance, and patience. They are Jim and Anna Byers of *The Man from Two Rivers*, in which Short also depicts anti-Indian prejudice in such a way as to put his Indians in a sympathetic light.[12] Occasionally a white character will make a shallow remark about Indians, who are thus characterized by generalization, not by action or direct speech of their own. For example, Pete Yard in *Brand of Empire* says with a laugh, " '. . .an Indian—any Indian—will tell you anything if he thinks you don't care about knowing it. They're the greatest gossips in the world' " (p. 67). Sam Kennery of *The Primrose Try* remembers "the Indian sense of timelessness. Where a white family man would come home at the end of his work day for supper and rest, the Indian ate when he was hungry and kept his own hours. The pattern of Indian life, Sam thought, was to have no pattern at all" (p. 82). Ward Kinsman's impassioned praise of the Apache way of life is memorable and features this central line: " 'I like the way Apaches live, and I think it's the way a man is meant to live' " (*Ambush*, p. 32).

V *Humor*

Short employs humor mainly as a characterizing device, rarely as a means of presenting setting, action, or meaning. All the same, in a quiet way, he can be immensely funny.[13]

His dramatis personae humorously characterize themselves by their own remarks, as savage, mordant, unsentimental, happy-go-lucky. Here is a little anthology of examples. " '. . .I was cussin' you so hard I sprained my tongue,' " and "I'll turn you over to rancher friends with evidence enough to hang you so high the birds can't get at you!' " (*Raiders of the Rimrock*, pp. 47, 100). " 'I'll twist your head off and run away with it and hide it' " *Bounty Guns*, p. 7). " 'You couldn't kick a mushroom over, Granpa. Don't brag' " (*Hardcase*, p. 59). " 'I could get awful sick of him' " (*Sunset Graze*, p. 29). " 'I would not contract to cut the posts to burn Jim Wade alive' " (*And the Wind Blows Free*, p. 24).

" 'Hell! If you want me to say I met a rider, I'll say it. But I didn't' " (*Station West*, p. 83). " 'They pair off nicely. . . . Give them three years and Larkin will have a greasy beard, he'll chew tobacco with his meals, and she'll be sewing him up in his underwear in the fall. . .' " (*High Vermilion*, p. 59). " '. . .I've never seen him come out the morning after a heavy drinkin' night and miss the saddle, like some of these [cavalry] officers' "; and " 'I wouldn't pet a dog until I've cleaned up' " (*Ambush*, pp. 94, 143). " 'If I'm to salute and jump off a cliff with no questions asked, I'd like to do it on salary' " (*Rimrock*, p. 94). ". . . I used to raise hell about four feet and tilt it every time I got the chance' " (*The Whip*, p. 45). " 'No ma'm, but you'd better stick to the planks crossing the [muddy] street or we're apt to lose you' " (*First Claim*, p. 112). " 'That crew would eat their young for a Confederate dollar. . . ,' " and " 'If you can't lick the teacher, you better study or quit school' " (*First Campaign*, pp. 7, 14).

Short often makes harshly humorous remarks in his own voice, or rather his unnamed narrator's or perhaps within an unspeaking character's mind—at any rate, not in dialogue. "She wouldn't even like him on Christmas" (*Barren Land Showdown*, p. 75). "If the cable bit through the rope too fast he had a drop that would break every bone in his body. They could bury him in a fry pan" (*Hardcase*, p. 88). "The big building was a hotel of sorts; it served meals that a man could forget in the bar that opened off the dining room. . ."; and "*There are worse things than work*, she thought bitterly" (*Play a Lone Hand*, pp. 54, 60). "Chuck Daily was better-dressed [for his victim's funeral] than he had been since the last time he wore a baby's dress" (*Last Hunt*, p. 59). "She was a woman of fifty and her ravaged, once-pretty face now held all the warmth of a prairie blizzard" (*First Campaign*, p. 130). ". . .[A] lanky and surly woman with greying hair so tightly drawn in a knot that it raised her eyebrows" (*Paper Sheriff*, pp. 110-11). "A drink of whiskey, if only to wash his teeth, would be a welcome thing" (*The Deserters*, p. 17). And "He removed the dead cigar from his mouth, revealing a chewed-up cud of tobacco the size of a child's fist" (*The Outrider*, p. 11).[14]

Short casually puns every once in a while—so unobtrusively, however, that I am not certain whether he is dead-pan ingenious or the puns are accidental. For example, some time after the hero of *Sunset Graze* fails to shoot the villain Arnie Chance, he says, " 'I missed my chance' " (p. 54). Later, the hero asks his ally to clear out and save himself; but that stalwart "comfortably" answers, " 'No chance' " (p. 140), meaning both that he is not a deserter and also, cryptically, that they have not yet destroyed Chance. The chapter in which the hero shoots villainous Major Fitz in *King Colt* is entitled "A Major Killing" (p. 178).[15] When the hero in *Raiders of the Rimrock* is outmaneuvered by the villainous sheepmen, we read that "He felt a little sheepish now" (p. 14). The hero of *The Whip*, Will Gannon, is praised for being able to "summon. . .his will power" (p. 72).[16] Jim Young of *Ride the Man Down* is seriously said to have a "young face" (p. 150). Only one Short hero consciously puns; he is Sam Dana of *Trouble Country*, who, after his ranch has been torched to charred embers by his vicious half-brother, is light-hearted enough to say to a girl offering sympathy, " 'It's done. . . . Very well done, if I can make a bad joke' " (p. 39).

Only two comic scenes exist in all of Short, both in late works. In *Man from the Desert*, Ben Kittrick in front of Carrie, one of his sisters, tries to rebuke the hero Hal Hanaway:

"Well, Hanaway, which of my sisters is going to marry you?"

Hanaway looked down at Carrie. Her lips parted in surprise at the question, she shifted her glance from Ben to Hanaway.

His face contained, Hanaway was silent a few seconds, thinking how Ben's question was put. Then he said soberly, "Which sister is going to marry me? I don't know yet, Ben. Up to now neither one has asked me for my hand. They's both nice girls, but I'll have to say no to one of them, won't I?"

Laughter exploded from Carrie. When she could talk, she choked out, still laughing, "You're so beautiful, Hal. Will you marry me?"

Laughing too, Hanaway looked down and scuffed the ground with his boot in mock shyness. "This is too quick, Carrie. Will you give me time to think it over?"

Ben roared angrily, "Goddamnit, stop that!"

This brought a fresh howl of laughter from Carrie. His own shoulders shaking in silent laughter, Hanaway looked at Ben. His sweaty face was livid with anger. (p. 84)

And in *The Man from Two Rivers*, Stacey and Anna, the latter an eloquent Indian woman, stage an insult to a disreputable white man at their boardinghouse by having Anna feign knowledge of only the most rudimentary English. " 'Me paid to work in house, not in barn' " (p. 74). The scene continues amusingly. But its light tone gives way a page later to its dreadful opposite, as charming Anna becomes the victim of a ferocious attempted rape.[17]

VI *Verisimilitude*

As we have seen, Short sketches in his settings with skill and dash. Never are they obtrusive; never, either, are they inaccurate. He does not show off with strings of accurate details, however, because his purpose was never to lecture his readers on Western American history. Rather, his purpose was to entertain them with breakneck action stories. All the same, reading his complete works can teach anyone a great deal about Western seaport activities, mining life, wagon and stagecoach work, railroading, the cattle industry, town life in the Old West, army duty on the frontier of the West and Southwest, the fate of Indians, Western law, and certain miscellaneous aspects of Western life.

Just as it was not Short's primary purpose to be informative, so is it not mine here to show in detail how verisimilar his works really are. That would be the job of a Western historian or perhaps only a sociogeological anthropologist. But a few general statements, many of which will be reminiscent of points already hinted at and situations already touched upon, may be helpful here.

The seaport area in the Gulf of California, at the mouth of the Colorado River, is sketched briefly in *Desert Crossing*, as cargo destined for Ehrenburg and Yuma is offloaded from a schooner. We follow some of the cargo by passenger steamer to Ehrenburg, where we see stevedores of three colors. This introductory action quickly ends, and the plot moves into the desert.

Short casts several novels in mining regions. The best are *Hard Money, High Vermilion,* and *The Outrider;* but in others as well he reveals detailed knowledge of gold, silver, copper, lead, coal and uranium—in the ground, on the surface, being blasted and dug for, tunneled to, fought over, and so on. Never does Short show off or intimidate the reader with excessive details or a specialized vocabulary. If he has to define an unusual word, he normally does so in conversation.

Vehicles drawn by horses or mules in Short are usually either ore wagons or stagecoaches. Once again, professional processes are revealed naturally. Most detailed information on ore-hauling comes in *Dead Freight for Piute.* Will Gannon of *The Whip* is a stage-line manager par excellence. In several other Short novels, transportation of these two kinds is significantly relied on.

Railroads figure in few of Short's novels, most notably in *Bold Rider, Three for the Money,* and *Man from the Desert.* Only in the last are construction details provided, while in all three, facts are subordinated to the exigencies of plot.

A modern reader anxious to learn what the whole Western cattle industry was like from about 1866 to 1896 could hardly do better than read the pertinent twenty-odd Short novels.[18] He would learn, in an enjoyably indirect way, about buying cattle down south *(And the Wind Blows Free),* driving them *(Gunman's Chance, Paper Sheriff),* roundup activities *(Vengeance Valley),* winter difficulties *(Sunset Graze, And the Wind Blows Free),* rustling and other violence *(The Branded Man, War on the Cimarron, Ride the Man Down, Sunset Graze, Paper Sheriff),* sheepman rivals *(Raiders of the Rimrock, Ramrod),* nesters and homesteaders opposing cattle barons and smaller cowboys *(First Claim, The Some-Day Country, Saddle by Starlight, Donovan's Gun),* selling beef to the Indians *(Gunman's Chance, And the Wind Blows Free),* and so on. Short knew his historical facts thoroughly, but he always subordinated them to his gripping yarn.

Short gives us the smell and feel of town life in the old days out West, especially in hotels, saloons, dance halls and their sometimes adjacent "cribs," and news and law offices. Curiously, we find no detailed scenes cast in churches or schools.[19]

Short's researches into army life out West were extensive, but the effects thereof are minimal and hazy in those few works featuring the military. The most informative are *And the Wind Blows Free, Ambush, Station West,* and *The Deserters.* Details of army uniforms, post life, discipline, unit identifications, and combat are exact but incidental. And readers are more concerned with Apaches, civilian criminals, and possibly even the love interest in these novels than they are in military trivia.

If a Western buff wants fiction in which Indians play a major role, he should stick with Zane Grey, Ernest Haycox, Henry Wilson Allen, Frank Waters, and Louis L'Amour, among others, and avoid Short. True, Indian men and women appear in a dozen of his novels; but rarely are they noble, presented in detail, or active for long. If Charles Marion Russell could have read Short's works, he might have agreed to illustrate only the following scenes with Indians: the beef issue in *And the Wind Blows Free*, the hero spying on Diablito's camp in *Ambush*, the army attacking the warned Apaches in *Summer of the Smoke*, and above all Sam Kennery's riding onto the Indian reservation in *The Primrose Try* and knowing "from long experience that the news of his presence here would precede him by moccasin telegraph" (p. 82).

Smacking of the truth are numerous details which Short's largesse incidentally lavishes about such diverse legal matters as Hispanic-American land claims (*Savage Range*), leasing Indian lands (*And the Wind Blows Free, The Some-Day Country*), renegade Indians' rights (*Ambush, Summer of the Smoke, The Primrose Try*), homesteaders' and nesters' legitimate rival claims (*Brand of Empire, Savage Range, Play a Lone Hand, Saddle by Starlight, The Some-Day Country, Donovan's Gun*), lawmen's conflicting jurisdictions (*The Guns of Hanging Lake, The Deserters, Man from the Desert, The Stalkers, Trouble Country*), the naming of state officials in a governor's temporary absence out of state (*The Outrider*), mine-leasing and related laws (*Hard Money, High Vermilion, Silver Rock, Rimrock, The Outrider*), recording easements (*Silver Rock*), and even the legality of poker debts (*Donovan's Gun*).

Finally, Short demonstrates his expertise in minor matters as well. Two areas come to mind, in addition to the several already hinted at. They are details of a geological nature, with which his prose often glitters unobtrusively (best in *Hard Money, Raw Land,* and *Rimrock*), and minutiae concerning horses.[20] I wish I could add that Short wrote like an expert in the realm of firearms, but he did not.[21]

CHAPTER 8

Short's Artistry (2)

REMAINING to be analyzed are Short's sense of structure, his use of various unifying devices, his language, infelicities in his composition, special stylistic charms, and his use of generalizations.

I *Structure*

Short is not a subtle fictive architect. His overriding formal virtue is his fast narrative pace. He generally starts a given novel with a bang and then continues with ever-increasing suggestions of suspense and excitement to a pounding climax and abrupt denouement. Occasionally he uses the flashback technique— often to present needed background information with dispatch, rarely with an effect of tedium. The artistic shape of a typical Short novel may be compared to a horse race between a hero and a villain (or members of the latter's wild crew), with obstacles and hidden ambuscades along the way, and with reward, love, and death at the finish line. We may also compare the action of a Short novel to war, chess, and poker. But Short's plots so closely resemble rival captains' actions in combat zones and parcels of no-man's land that they are less like declared war than a form of guerrilla action or civilian mayhem. The comparison to the contours of chess games is limited: there may be kings, knights, and pawns aplenty; but queens and bishops are few, and even more seldom do we hear the warning cry of "Check." However, Short's heroes and villains do closely resemble skillful poker players—knowing when to stand pat, when to draw, and certainly when to bet, bluff, and call.

Short is one of the tightest plotters on record. But all the same, he does present an occasional digression and even a subplot or two. Thus we have hero and villain in *Bold Rider* reminiscing about when their pasts converged, we have the Ulibarri land grant background in more detail than is strictly needful in *Savage Range*, we enjoy the marvelous Opera House digression in *Hard Money*, we learn about the flawed heroine's ebullient great-aunt (long dead) in *And the Wind Blows Free*, and we grimace at distant background details of the smelly Fasken clan in *Vengeance Valley*. Close to subplot status are the romances of Will Racklin and Catherine Henry in *The Some-Day Country*, and Ted Elser and Carol Lufton in *Gunman's Chance*, among a few others.

Harmonizing the design of a typical Short novel is contrapuntal rhythm. The tedium of the law's delay is jostled by the furious frenzy of the hero's gallop to justice or vengeance. If a person tends to speak too slowly, an impatient listener will nudge him on, as Buck Tolleston does Mitch Budrow in *Marauders' Moon*, for instance, when the two talk. Repeatedly, we read that a central character's musings, ponderings, queryings of fate are nullified by the quick jerk back to attention to the present danger by a word, a sound, a danger. The hero often pauses for a smoke. Short does not often use the device of ominsciently shifted scenes; but, when he chooses to do so, he can be most effective, as in *The Stalkers*, in which Chapters 14, 16, and 18 start with the focus on the hero, while Chapters 15 and 17 focus on the villain. Likewise, many examples could be cited to show that Short typically moves his action from town to country and back again.

II   *Unity of Time and Place*

Short unifies his action by speeding up time. As in many of Shakespeare's history plays, given sequences of events in Short's works happen faster than they could in real life. For example, on one page of *The Feud at Single Shot* (p. 139), the hero's comic sidekick gets the sheriff to have the prosecuting attorney hire the other two town lawyers for other work so that they cannot counsel the villain, learns that all has been done as suggested, ascertains that the villain has checked into the local hotel, sends for him, and observes him as he descends the stairs. Far more complex action occurs in a matter of hours in *King Colt, Debt of Honor*, and *The Deserters*. Further, beat-up heroes and villains heal in a matter of days if plot requirements call for them to do so. For a few examples, John Haven of *Station West* and Will Christie of *The Outrider,* and Loosh Petrie of *The Branded Man* and Keen Billings of *Dead Freight for Piute,* all do. I feel confident that Rita of *Trouble Country,* in spite of her broken jaw, nose, and cheek, will be ready for her honeymoon with the hero in a matter of hours following his last-page proposal. (And this in spite of the doctor's insistence that she needs three weeks to recuperate.)

The desire to use the unity of time also impels Short to compress climactic action, especially in several of the late novels, into a matter of a few specified days. Time is particularly tight in *Hard Money, Gunman's Chance,* and *High Vermilion,* since their respective heroes must work against definite legal deadlines.[1] But it is breathlessly constricted in Short's last six books, especially *Three for the Money.* Chapter 1 of that brilliantly plotted novel[2] occurs on a Monday, with prologuelike action. Chapters 2–4 introduce us to the hero, Cam Holgate, as he rides into town one week later (perhaps the next Monday?), looking into reward-money details and then having a busy, dangerous day and night. Chapters 5–13 all take place the following day (Tuesday?), in an orderly sequence—morning, noon, early afternoon, mid-afternoon, an hour later, and then back to noon so that we may watch the bumbling sheriff in his office. Chapter 14 occurs the next dawn (Wednesday?). Then Chapter 15 returns to the previous night, so that we may eavesdrop on one set of villains—Crowder and his gang. Chapter 16 continues the action of the day which began in Chapter 14, and the sun is low in the west as the climax of the whole novel occurs. Chapter 17, the final one, takes place late the same day and features the denouement. It may be only Wednesday.

Short is even more specific in *Trouble Country,* although I think he is less accurate. He starts the action on a Saturday (Chapters 1–2). It continues apace on Sunday (Chapter 3[3]); then come Monday (Chapters 4, 5), Tuesday (Chapter 6), Wednesday (Chapter 7), and Thursday (Chapter 8). Here, I think Short may have become confused; evidence of no great moment points to the conclusion that the action of Chapter 9 and part of Chapter 10 occurs on Friday, but the next day is surely Friday (Chapter 10).[4] In any event, Chapters 10 and 11 take place on Friday; Chapter 12, on Saturday; Chapter 13, Sunday (with a bit of quiet, if essential, town action) and then Monday. After this, time backs

up to Saturday again (Chapter 14) so that we may shadow the
villain into his hiding place. Then time jerks forward, as we
follow that unsavory scoundrel through Sunday and on—
uncertainly—perhaps to Wednesday or later (Chapter 15). The
final day of the action is the next day (Chapter 17).

Short occasionally turns the clock back a little, as we have just
seen, to pick up previously unreported but essential action. He
rarely does so awkwardly, and never as a result of thoughtless or
insufficient planning. In fact, even in less tightly calendared plots
he sometimes does so, for the purpose of showing another
character's different responses to an identical, already-reported
event. Thus in *Bounty Guns* we follow the hero's escape from an
attempted in-jail ambush; then we see the same action again
from a would-be bushwhacker's point of view (pp. 122–25). This
technique is effectively cinematic. Or Short turns back the
clock—à la Virginia Woolf—to show what a character or a set of
characters was doing at the moment of some previously
delineated action—often noisy action. For example, in *Dead
Freight for Piute* the shout of " 'Fire! Fire! Everybody out!' "
interrupts Cole and Letty; then time backs up, so that we may
read about Billings and Linton, whose ponderings on the
unknown villain's activities are interrupted by " 'Fire! All out!
The Monarch's on fire!' " (pp. 78, 80).[5]

In addition to occasionally turning back the narrative clock,
Short sometimes stops it altogether, to let his readers catch their
breath while a character summarizes bewildering action in his
own mind. Examples are frequent; in fact, the little technical
trick becomes almost a mannerism, and one extremely helpful to
the sometimes puzzled reader. Thus we read in *Savage Range*
that "alone, picking his way through the cedars, alert for any
sound, Jim took stock of his fortunes so far. . . . Scoville's advent
was plain luck. Jim had taken him to Cope's and ordered him to
shave his beard. Here was a man who. . .could [now] circulate
without drawing suspicion. . . . But with only Scoville and a
green kid, he had to buck Bonsell's crew and Cruver's. Could he
do it? And the image of Mary rose in his mind to strengthen him
and confound him" (pp. 85, 86).[6]

Sometimes Short ticks off the difficulties surrounding an
oppressed villain. Thus Tate Riling of *Gunman's Chance* at one
point surveys his gunnies, recalls his past, and in the process
unconsciously employs narrative foreshadowing: "He looked

them over, and it gave him a sick feeling. He'd started out with a dozen men. Riordan was dead; Sweet was dead; Shotten was useless; Garry had deserted; Fred Barden was dead, and Anse Barden had high-tailed it. That left seven, counting himself, and he was taking two of them with him. Four men to hold Lufton— and not one of them mad enough to risk his neck" (p. 157).

Most of these devices—tight plotting, speeding up the time of action, compressing it into hours rather than days or days rather than weeks, turning back the clock, and recapitulating—relate to the Aristotelian unity of time, so valued in taut drama and story.[7] Short also obeys the precepts of those who theorize in favor of the unity of place. The place in Short's works is usually the Old West or the Old Southwest. His typical hero starts somewhere, moves through dangerous if not changing terrain, and emerges a winner, richer and loved. We are never in ignorance of the layout of a given region, even though it may be a montage of real places which Short knew intimately, rather than a specific place.

The neatest little example of unity of place in Short appears in *Silver Rock*, which begins with Tully Gibbs entering the mining town of Azurite on a moonless night by train, and ends shortly after he returns on the same train from an evidence-gathering visit to nearby Galena. The coincidence is not lost on Tully: ". . .He was about to swing up the [passenger-car] steps when the brakeman descended. It was the same brakeman who'd been on duty when Tully first hit Azurite, and he recognized Tully" (p. 142).[8] The pendulum in several of Short's novels swings from one town to another and back again, and in a manner providing rhythmical unity. In *High Vermilion*, the two towns are Vermilion and Weed; in *Rimrock*, Ute City, Colorado, and Joash, Utah; in *First Campaign*, Junction City and Primrose; and in *The Deserters*, Banning and Indian Bend, with special cleverness.

III   *Foreshadowing and Nonverbal Communication*

Two relatively minor devices which Short employs to rein-force the unity of his fictive designs are foreshadowing and nonverbal communication. For example, he leads us to believe that John Haven will love Mary Iles eventually *(Station West)*, that the immigrant wagons often mentioned early may prove useful to Will Gannon later *(The Whip)*, that the stink of Seeley Carnes's rank tobacco will give him away one day *(The Primrose*

Try), and that the professional predictions of Tim Sefton's recovery of memory should prove true before long *(The Stalkers).*

Somewhat more subtle is Short's use of body language and allied forms of symbolic communication. When in *Hardcase* the villain deliberately scratches fine furniture with his sharp spurs, he is not only expressing his contempt for the Establishment but also revealing his quintessential crumminess. More significantly, Short at one point in *Ride the Man Down* has Will Ballard's sexual rival Sam Danfelser "cease. . .his pacing in the exact center of the pattern on the [heroine's] living-room carpet"; then a page later we read that "Will didn't look at Sam, didn't answer him. He came out into the middle of the room, facing her, his big shoulders a little stooped, and he was waiting. . ." *(Ride the Man Down,* pp. 61, 62). The men are beginning to vie for centrality in Celia Evarts's old residence and new life. More blatant is this: when the hero mounts the veranda steps to approach the heroine, we read that "Ann Dunnifon sat in a rocker, her legs crossed; now she uncrossed them and smoothed her skirt, and. . ." *(Ambush,* p. 42).

Gestures are frequent in Short's narratives. Men dry-scrub their stubbled faces with gnarled hands, gesticulate palms up to indicate something or other, walk around desks to get nearer to potential adversaries, shrug expressively, and cuff back their Stetsons[9] in exasperation or fatigue. They roll, make, or build cigarettes, smoke and chew cigars (especially early in Short's career), and offer them to possible opponents as a gesticulatory time-killer. Indians and some white men who have long associated with them point with their chins too often to tabulate. Short's women are usually more passive, but a rather common gesture is the habit of at least a dozen of them of folding their arms across their breasts. The motion may unconsciously symbolize both resistance to the male stare and a psychological fending off of any possible closer approach.

IV *Language*

Fully as much as Aeschylus, Virgil, Shakespeare, Milton, and Melville, though more modestly, Luke Short has a vocabulary of his own.

Aside from the simplest, the words and phrases which Short

uses most often are the following: "accept" (as in "The horse accepted its rider"), "achieve" (as in "He achieved the crest of the hill"), "affair" (for building), "arrogance," "bafflement," "barrel chair" (almost every veranda in Short's West has at least a few), "batwings" (the swinging door of a saloon), "to beat [or flog] one's mind," "beef [or buffalo]" (knock unconscious), "bench" (flat place on a hill), "bisect" (as in "a sweeping moustache bisected his face"), "bleach-eyed" (only in villains), "boil out" (rush out), "bray" (the sound made by a villain when slugged in the gut), "build [or fashion]" (that is, roll, as a cigarette), "cedar-handled" (many early guns in Short are so fitted), *chamiso*, "choose him" (call him out to shoot him), *cienega*, "clean range clothes" (often with half-boots), "comb him out" (rebuke him), "coony" (cannily resourceful), "crib" (brothel room), "cross-legged" (or "tailor fashion," "Indian fashion"—a way of sitting), "cuff [or prod, thumb]" (push back, as a Stetson), "cull [or jag]" (inferior cattle, often strays), "cut down on" (draw a gun on, menacingly), "cut sign" (cross a track or trail), "cut your dogs loose" (go ahead and attack), "dead-white hair" (as on aging villains), "dodger" (wanted poster), "drag it" (get moving), "drily [dryly]" "false dawn" (also "full dawn"), "feral," "fiddlefoot," "fog it" (hurry), "fort up" (prepare to resist an expected attack), "full-bodied" (as in atractive young women), "gaunted" (fined down, leaned down), "glass it" (survey it with binoculars), "grain him" (feed my horse grain, and be quick about it), "gray" (used to describe a somber feeling, prospect, or thought), "greener" (shotgun), "grin around" (see "speak around"), "gulch" (transitive verb), "gunny" (unsavory hired gun or armed cohort).

And "hack at" (nag), "heel" (tilt over, as in "the sun was heeling over now"), "hipshot" (said of ponies and horses), "hone for" (anticipate eagerly, usually used in the negative), "honky-tonk" (adjective used to describe a low woman), "hungrily" (lustfully), "hunker" (squat down), "impatience" (see "patience"), "Indian" (canny, patient, resourceful, vindictive, as in "He's too Indian for me"), "insolent," "jasper" (a no-good fellow), "jerk [yank]" (as in "Her voice yanked his mind back to their plight"), "knuckle-studded" (as in "He smashed him with knuckle-studded blows"), "law" (transitive verb, as in "Don't try to law me"), "lift" (as in "He lifted his horse into a gallop," "lifted his glance," "the land lifted now"), "lie" (untruth), "light

a shuck" (hightail it out), "loads" (bullets, shells), "lounge erect,"
malpais, "meager" (usually in "a meager smile"), "melt" (drop
suddenly and quietly, often fatally, as in "He melted out of the
saddle," "he melted to the floor"), "mile-eating" (as in "a mile-
eating trot"), "mixed train" (freight and passenger cars
together), "motte," "nail one's hide" (catch and punish one),
"near" (for nearly, as in "near hopeless," "near dark"), "nooned"
(stopped at noon), "offsaddled," "on the dodge," "on the prod"
(i.e., "proddy"), "palm [palm up]" (as in "He palmed the
doorknob," "palmed up his gun"), *pasear* [*passear*], "paste" (as
in "He had a wet cigar pasted in his mouth"), "patience" (now
see "vast"), "pinwheel" (what lights do when one is slugged
hard), "pound sand" (waste time), "purely" (as in "I purely hated
this"), "puzzlement," "raffish," "rake" (as in "He raked his
glance across . . ."), "ranahan [ranny]" (jasper), "rataplan" (a
beating sound, as in gunfire), "rawhide" (chew out, rebuke),
"redheaded" (obstreperous, as in "Don't get redheaded with
me"), *remuda*, "ribbon" (as in "His thoughts ribboned back to
the time when . . ."), "ride" (fret), "ride the river with" (highly
complimentary, as in "He'll do to ride the river with"), "riffraff,"
rincon, "rough lock" (the beginning of a hold or solution), "run a
sandy" (deceive).

And also "saddle of hair" (that is, partly bald), "seep" (noun),
segundo, "shelf" (part of jaw frequently treated to knuckle-
studded fists), "shrug" (into or out of, as with shirts), "shoot to
doll rags" (shoot full of holes), "shuttle" (as one's glance), "side"
(transitive verb, as in "I expect you to side me"), "skyline"
(transitive verb, as in "Skyline them, then shoot 'em"), "slack"
(usually into a chair, as in "He slacked into the nearest barrel
chair wearily"), "sock feet," "some" (somewhat, as in "That
happened some later"), "sound-shooting" (shooting in the
direction of a disliked person's noise), "speak around [or grin
around]" (done when one's mouth is full, of food, cigar, pipe,
cigarette, match, or toothpick, as in "He grinned around his wet
cigar"), "stayer" (durable horse), "stippled" (as in "the cedar-
stippled slope"), "stuffed Stetson" (a stupid cowboy, cattle
baron, sheepman, or Western lawyer), "sun-blackened"
(tanned), "surly," "swivel" (turn quickly, as in "He swiveled his
head to lift a surly glance"), "take water" (back down under
pressure), "tawny," "thinly," "tilt" (as in "Now the land began to
tilt"), "toll" (transitive verb, lure on a pretense, as in "He tolled

them out of town"), "turn up" (inform on), "understrapper" (hireling), "utterly," "vast" (adjective overused to modify both "impatience" and "patience"), "wash" (as in "Anger washed over him"), "wench" (an insulting term), "whippoorwill" (stupid enemy), "wipe" (somewhat like melt, as in "The shotgun blast wiped him out of the saddle"), "wipe a light" (strike, as a match for a cigar or arson), "wolf" (as in "They wolfed their meal"), and "woolly" (irate).

Obviously, few of the above words and phrases are unusual. Many may be found in Western writings by others. But the frequency with which Short uses them, as well as the combinations he makes out of many of them, give his works a unique timbre and a savory smack.

V *Composition Errors*

Short is often careless and hasty. Perhaps he read Thomas Hardy's advice: "The whole secret of a living style, and the difference between it and a dead style, lies in not having too much style—being in fact a little careless, or rather seeming to be, here and there."[10] In any event, Short is often "in fact a little careless." His commonest errors are dangling modifiers, absence of parallelism, grammatical mistakes, and minor infelicities in syntax and idiom.

Of about two hundred danglers, the following are among the most blatant: "Inquiring of the hostler if Carnes was boarding a horse there, the horse was pointed out to him" (*The Primrose Try*, p. 128). " 'Being a woman, I [Hobart Carew] suppose you'll want a church wedding' " (*The Man from Two Rivers*, p. 122). "In Sam's absence, leaving no instructions, it was pretty much his own choice" (*Trouble Country*, p. 80). Alongside some danglers, and often in the same paragraph, are correct participial constructions.

Examples of grammatical elements juxtaposed out of parallel abound in Short. Here are some obvious little ones: "Hand either thought the time was too short to wait for reinforcements, or he had forgotten them" (*The Branded Man*, p. 46). "There, around the timberline, it would not only be rocky and therefore difficult to track in, but the timber would thin out. . ." (*The Guns of Hanging Lake*, p. 48). "Austin didn't bother to either thank him or to carry out the drinks" (*Trouble Country*, p. 55). The last quoted example also contains a split infinitive—not a serious nor a rare error in Short, who once also managed to combine a dangling modifier with an unparallel construction: "Being both a gregarious and curious man, Cass's first impulse was to ask Mary why she wasn't at work. . ." *(Play a Lone Hand,* p. 132). And so on.

Short often uses "whom" incorrectly, the way many fast writers do who strive for hyper-correctness. "The night after the funeral Jess Gove, whom he, along with everybody else, believed was next thing to a saint, had called him in" *(Sunset Graze,* p. 87); "both men and women whom she thought had overheard" *(The Some-Day Country,* p. 96); "a full-figured woman whom he guessed would be in her late thirties" *(First Campaign,* p. 161). And so on.

Akin to "who-whom" errors is the misuse of "who" for "which," as in "tracks of cattle who" *(Raiders of the Rimrock,* p. 75), "the dozen horses who" *(The Whip,* p. 24). And so on.

The "who" in each of the ensuing constructions is followed by an incorrect singular verb instead of a correct plural one: " 'The man over there in that cell is one of three or four men who's kept it goin' " *(Bounty Guns,* p. 61); "one of the girls who was finishing setting the tables" *(Coroner Creek,* p. 73); " '. . .one of the few women I know who's scared' " *(Silver Rock,* pp. 76–77). Like most normal Americans, Short's characters and Short misuse "lay" for "lie," as in " 'I'll bet it's layin' in his back room' " *(Marauders' Moon,* pp. 111–12), and "The chuck wagon was laying on its side" *(War on the Cimarron,* p. 21).

Short often violates the rule that a pronoun and its antecedent, and a subject and its verb, should agree in number. The useless expletive or so-called function word "there" comes in for tedious overuse throughout Short's fiction. Short also had trouble with "between" constructions (" 'hard feeling between almost every man in this room' " [*Brand of Empire,* p. 58]), and minor syntactical and idiomatic problems, such as "cannot help but do," "farthest" of two, "latter" of three, "the reason is because," "providing" instead of "provided," and others. His haste in composition, desire to write mainly for the masses, and lack of good editors led him into errors which ninety-nine out of a hundred of his readers never notice.[11] So enough of this graceless ticking off of peccadilloes in an author with as much creativity and energy as a dozen carping pedagogues.

VI *Stylistic Charms*

Short is admirable for spinning terse phrases, in describing physical sensations (especially smells and sounds), and in fashioning simple similes and metaphors. He also can get a trifle salty in his lingo at times.

The following are neatly epigrammatical phrases: "aggressive friendliness," "angry wariness," "belligerent petulance," "brash glee," "concentrated reticence" (of poker players), "jaunty laziness," "mountain anger," "nameless grief blotting out all thought" (reminiscent of Montaigne), "ruthless dignity," "sensuous secretiveness," "stern optimism," "sullen indecision," "tin-pot Messiah," "wary curiosity," and "withering malevolence."

Smells which Short describes with unusual pungency are of elements of nature outdoors, man's heavy work, human filth, and sultry women. Examples: "In this bright morning with the tang of fall in the air, with the close Rafts ablaze with color and the good smell of warming sage in the air" (*First Campaign*, p. 44). "The slow wind rustled her skirts, and she smelled the warm summer scent of wind on grass and the faint smoky odor of cedar" (*Raw Land*, p. 111). "He waited, watching the hotel, smelling the warm dust of the street and the faint ammoniac smell of manure around the watering trough by the cottonwood nearby" (*Ramrod*, pp. 213-14). "Bolling. . .opened the door, the hot smell of dust and grease and leather drifting out" (*Bounty Guns*, p. 85). "There was a stench of burned hoof, hot iron and coal smoke that hung persistently in the shed" (*Vengeance Valley*, p. 45). "Inside, the halls were lofty and dim-lit and smelled of aged wood and well-used cuspidors" (*Silver Rock*, pp. 8-9). ". . .Reese entered the mean single room. . .[which] was airless and stank of unwashed clothes and fried food" (*Paper Sheriff*, p. 66). "When he passed by Will, his body gave off the reek of a goat" (*The Outrider*, p. 147). "As the church filled with miners, the stink of sweat, sour clothes, unwashed bodies and stale alcohol was so overpowering that Will breathed through his mouth" (ibid., p. 27). Hutch Forney says that his Indian wife is "'black-eyed and coffee-colored and smelling like a bonfire'" (*The Whip*, p. 34). But "When Tenney spoke she seemed very close to him; he even caught a pleasant smell of newly washed, sun-dried hair" (*The Primrose Try*, p. 57).

Short's most crackling sounds have to do with horses and

gunfire. "Presently Webb heard the soft *hush, hush* of a horse traveling in sand" *(Marauders' Moon,* p. 60). And "It came presently—the sound of a horse walking. Bill listened intently; a stray horse feeling is easily distinguishable in the sounds it makes from a ridden horse, and Bill listened for the broken rhythm of its walk. This horse, he soon knew, was being ridden" *(Ramrod,* p. 192).

As for bullets—"The futile rifles hammered at them all day long, their slugs whistling harmlessly off into the blue" *(Savage Range,* p. 125); and ". . .the second shot ricocheted off into the darkness with a whine" *(Donovan's Gun,* p. 89). On occasion, a faraway shot will "echo battering up through the timber" *(Ramrod,* p. 195). Shots closer to home drum, hit, lace, racket, slap, and so on.

About the only tastes Short concentrates on are those of tobacco and kisses. His men mostly "wolf" their food and toss off cheap whiskey without particularly savoring either. But tobacco—"Cass lighted his pipe and watched a minute, savoring the raw raking shock of the tobacco in his lungs" *(Fiddlefoot,* p. 61). And kisses—"Her lips seemed to dissolve wetly against his" *(Donovan's Gun,* p. 106); "Her body was soft against his and her lips were warm and loose and sweet," and again "Her lips were warm and moist and tantalizing and Cam gently disengaged her arms. . ." *(Three for the Money,* pp. 31, 59).[12]

Short rarely indulges in synaesthetic imagery, but here are two instances: ". . .she was so close to him that he could smell the warmth of her" *(Savage Range,* p. 23), and "Heth waited the second it took for the gun flash to wash out of his eyes. . ." *(Saddle by Starlight,* p. 152).

Figurative imagery in Short is basic but effective. Pain, anger, fatigue regularly wash over his heroes,[13] who are also drugged by enervating experiences. Their gunfire is regularly a blossom of orange flame. Resolution and will power, among other attributes in tough-fibered heroes, are often like iron. People of various sorts, good and bad, are likened to children with surprising frequency, while stubborn or skittish people are muley or coltish. Perhaps as many as a dozen big men, either heroes or otherwise, have eyes and jowls which Short feels he must liken to those of a hound dog. Over and over, he also images good smells and awful stinks as hitting someone's nostrils like a pillow. And, if the pervasive imagery is any indication, Short saw life not as a moveable feast but as a moveable poker game, with raw deals but also a handful of options.

Once in a while Short offers imagery which seems so elaborate and out of key as to appear forced. Thus, we have a cough "like gears meshing" (*Gunman's Chance*, p. 90), a slugged man's head seeming to be "loaded with marbles that rolled into a pocket above his eyes" (*Saddle by Starlight*, p. 143), a hypocrite's "periodic laugh. . .that. . .rang as false as an old maid's giggle" (*The Primrose Try*, pp. 12–13), and this admittedly spectacular effort: "The liquor unfurled in his stomach with a soft explosion" (*The Guns of Hanging Lake*, p. 111). Short's very earliest metaphor remains one of his most charming: ". . .countless stars semaphoring silently" (*The Feud at Single Shot*, p. 21).

Short is a remarkably clean writer, as most traditional Western-fiction authors are; but he does indulge in a few ribaldries. The most notable such sequence occurs in the relatively late novel *The Stalkers*, during which the prostitute Pearl on a bet strides naked into a presumably deserted street, only to hear her rivals from their windows across the street comment on her "muff" and "puppies" (p. 12). Obscenities and profanity are almost never made explicit in Short. Instead he typically hints in ways like this: "He laughed then and uttered a derisive obscenity" (*The Guns of Hanging Lake*, p. 88). True, Short stoops to an occasional "Jesus," "God damn," "son of a bitch,"[14] and . "bitch." But even the word "wench," now manifestly harmless and perhaps even endearing, was to Short's sensitive heroes' ears an insult calling for satisfaction by knightly suitor. Short is so sanitary that he doctors a well-known idiom to read thus: " 'Don't go off half cocked. Once you do, the pie has hit the fan' " (*Silver Rock*, p. 88).

In an age jaded by the writings of cheap followers of the magnificent D. H. Lawrence, James Joyce, and Sherwood Anderson, among other pioneers and liberators, it is refreshing to turn for pleasure and precept to works from the fierce clean pen of Luke Short.

VII *Generalizations*

Finally, we come to generalizations, a rhetorical device which Short employs with great effectiveness. Taken separately, they may not seem like much. But in combination, they comprise a piquant little handbook about men and women, youth and age, love and hate, and a way of life even now not totally beyond recall or partial emulation.

Short uses generalizations in two ways. Either a character is made to project an image of himself as vastly experienced and hence capable of generalizing on life tellingly, or a given unnamed narrator looks somewhat wearily at his puppets and comments on the wider significance of their puny activities and aspirations. A great number of Short's three hundred or so generalizations concern women, oddly enough—their hard lives (especially in the harsh Old West), their difficult relationships with men, their attitudes toward each other, and their intuitional powers, hopes, conversational abilities, best attributes, drinking habits, and appeal.

Short also generalizes on a myriad of male thoughts, traits, and acts: boasting, blackmailing, bullying, love of clothes, crimes, dare-taking, rejection and acceptance of aspects of death, duty, endurance and fatigue, fate and free will, friendship, greed, grudge-holding, respect for horses, justice, impatience, pity (including self-pity), power, pride, revenge, smugness and success, treachery, and wealth.

The image of Frederick Dilley Glidden which I have gradually developed in my mind after a close reading of his half a hundred gripping novels is one of a pragmatist (not in any sense an abstract philosopher), a stoic, a lover of nature, a male chauvinist (but a chivalric, gentle, level-headed, humorous one), and most importantly a man whom life did not make more sure of himself as time went on but instead more tentative in drawing conclusions. A majority of Short's generalized statements appear well before the midpoint of his writing career. The last dozen novels seem less assertive in this regard, more tentative. The novels which have the most generalizations are *Gunman's Chance*, then *Coroner Creek* and *Ambush*, followed by *And the Wind Blows Free* and *Last Hunt*. These are not late works.

Many of Short's cynical generalizations are memorable. Space permits the quoting of only a few here. Men: " 'Did you ever know a sister who thought any woman was good enough for her brother to marry?' " (*Donovan's Gun*, p. 49). " 'Even if a man isn't born to suffer like they tell us, he soon picks up the ability' " (*Hard Money*, p. 132). Women: "In his sight she was nothing, one of the people who should never have been born, a woman who would drudge out her days unwanted and unneeded. A man, Chuck reasoned, had independence and a few solid pleasures. This woman had nothing but a friendless old age to look forward to. . ."(*Last Hunt*, p. 20). "She knew they could have a good life together [without real love]; that was all, really, that a woman got out of this world" (*Ambush*, p. 99). Youth: " 'The young do foolish things' " (*Hardcase*, p. 45). "Worry was riding him [the young hero], Hutch [an old-timer] knew, and that wasn't good, but he supposed that was part of youth when ambition seemed so important" (*Rimrock*, pp. 98–99). Age: "Back of thought, he wondered with an old man's surfeit of life if he would ever have rest from trouble" (*Hard Money*, p. 76). "Jimmy had been all the old man [his father] had, and for a fleeting moment Tully sensed the ageless tragedy of the childless old" (*Silver Rock*, p. 5). Death: "This was the end of it, expressed in the oddly gentle mockery of the dead" (*High Vermilion*, p. 131). "It was the saddest part of life, that a father should see his son dead before him, she thought" (*First Claim*, p. 147).[15] Life in general: "The facts were plain enough and always had been; you fought your whole life if you wanted to live" (*Savage Range*, p. 17). " 'It's a rotten world, with rotten people in it' " (*Barren Land Showdown*, p. 151).[16] "Justice was a thing few people ever received from life" (*First Claim*, p. 21). "Whenever fate offered you a choice, it was between two bad things, never between a good or a bad thing" (*First Campaign*, p. 180). And, curiously, " 'One of the nicest things in life is to want something you don't deserve and know you'll never get it' " (*Man from the Desert*, p. 59).

Luke Short generalizes effectively on many other topics, but the above should sufficiently suggest his versatility, bracing cynicism,[17] and commendable, Melvillean honesty.

CHAPTER 9

A Craftsman Proud to Entertain

F RED GLIDDEN, better known by his pen name "Luke Short," regarded himself as an entertainer. He was a product of the Great Depression and a failed journalist. He began writing for the pulps in the mid-1930s because he had had theoretical training to write, rough adventures in the Southwest and in Canada to stimulate his imagination, and seemingly few other options. From the start he wrote to make money. Once he got an agent, he began to succeed with unbelievable speed. When he graduated to the slicks and then to hardbound-book publication, he was pleased, but only because doing so meant reaching a larger audience, entertaining more people, and hence earning more money. He tried to make it big in Hollywood and later in the television industry, for—again—more money.

Short succeeded phenomenally. In the late 1930s some pulps paid him only 2 cents a word.[1] But from 1940 through 1957, his agent forwarded $535,000 to him—and this sum exclusive of about $80,000 more from Hollywood.[2] In the 1950s his agent once advised him to forget chancy TV and stick to books, for which he could earn at least 33 cents a word.[3] He wrote 30,000 to 50,000 words a month at this point in his career, when the mood struck him. The 1960s and early 1970s were similarly secure financially. Bantam ultimately guaranteed him a minimum of $15,000 per original paperback novel.

Short felt competitive, but only on his terms. He enormously respected Eugene Manlove Rhodes and Ernest Haycox, felt that he could never better the latter's works, and would therefore have to "write around him," as he once put it to his agent.[4] As for certain rival *Saturday Evening Post* writers, Short once boasted to his agent that he could "outwrite. . .those guys with a crayon."[5] Authors whom his agent most frequently named to Short as threats to his eminence were James Warner Bellah, Max

Brand, Eugene Cunningham, Frank Gruber, Louis L'Amour, and that newcomer Jack Schaefer. Short himself mentioned Faulkner a few times in admiration and once thought his own short story "The Danger Hole" had the nostalgia of Eugene O'Neill's *Ah, Wilderness!*[6] An admirable professional trait Short often exhibited was concern for young authors trying to get a break; he often recommended them to his agent and once annoyed some bigwigs at the headquarters of one of his publishers by puffing a Western being published by a rival firm.[7]

Like most Western successes, Short was contemptuous of Eastern critics and once wrote that the popularity of Western fiction was too simple for "the professors, who are paid to think," to figure out. He then explained the mystery: Westerns are written by craftsmen proud to entertain.[8] Further, he wrote his agent shortly before her death that his papers (including letters from her), which he was then about to donate to the University of Oregon library, were of limited worth: "Actually, the only value to a university researcher [he graciously added] would be to show how a writer works hand in hand with a very good agent over a long time."[9] In reality, however, as I think we have seen, they show much more.

If Short was a slick producer, which I have demonstrated that he was, he was also, as he rightly boasts, a successful member of a proud craft. Following the primitivists, the dime novelists, and at least one full wave of early twentieth-century Western craftsmen, Short joined such other popular and talented writers of cowboy thrillers as Zane Grey, Max Brand, Ernest Haycox, Louis L'Amour, Henry Wilson Allen, and Jack Schaefer to produce some of the best, most authentic, and certainly tense examples of the undying genre.

Short handles his typical settings—the Rocky Mountain West and the vast desert Southwest—with matchless skill. He characterizes crisply and basically; his ruggedly individualistic heroes are particularly memorable, as are many of his lumpish villains and his smoldering heroines. His plots are elemental, close to the primeval, and link to world myth and legend compellingly. He praises courage, loyalty, courtesy, and tenacity, as exemplified by his go-to-hell, never-say-die heroes. His literary style, in spite of his antiacademic asides, can strike responding chords in readers behind moist ivy walls as well as those in the dusty great outdoors. Especially vivid are his primary painterly strokes—through unusual diction, rasping dialogue, structural unity, and so on—his glints of humor, and his frosty, cynical generalizations.

But what readers should remember longest about Luke Short's fiction is the pragmatic optimism of his composite hero: such a man sees what must be done, then does it. After all, when legal niceties threatened to hedge in Fred Glidden, Aspen councilman, he took the more direct line. Highway billboards were diminishing the beauty of the Aspen countryside? He obliterated them with paint mops. A friend's dying wish to have his ashes scattered over their beloved town ran counter to some silly local ordinance? Fred gave moral support to those who chartered a plane and scattered them there anyway. In his way, mild-mannered Frederick D. Glidden acted out aspects of his fiction and, I hope, became his own Western hero.

Notes and References

Chapter One

1. See James K. Folsom, "novel, western," p. 850, in *The Reader's Encyclopedia of the American West* (New York, 1977).
2. Mis-explanation of the West for Eastern readers is the subject of Robert Edson Lee, *From West to East: Studies in the Literature of the American West* (Urbana, Ill., 1966).
3. See Daryl Jones, *The Dime Novel Western* (Bowling Green, Ohio, 1978).
4. See Russel Nye, *The Unembarrassed Muse: The Popular Arts in America* (New York, 1970), pp. 283–87.
5. See Kent L. Steckmesser, *The Western Hero in History and Legend* (Norman, Okla., 1965), *passim;* Nye, *The Unembarrassed Muse,* pp. 281–83, 285, 287; and Bruce A. Rosenberg, *Custer and the Epic of Defeat* (University Park, Penna., 1974).
6. See Daniel J. Boorstin, *The Americans: The Democratic Experience* (New York, 1973), pp. 5–41 passim.
7. See Richard W. Etulain, "The Historical Development of the Western," *Journal of Popular Culture,* 7 (Winter 1973), 719.
8. See Nye, *The Unembarrassed Muse,* pp. 290–93.
9. Ibid., pp. 293–97.
10. John G. Cawelti, *Adventure, Mystery, and Romance: Formula Stories as Art and Popular Culture* (Chicago and London, 1976), p. 9.
11. Nye, *The Unembarrassed Muse,* p. 298.
12. Who was not included? In 1951, 35 million copies of Western novels were sold, or 16 percent of all paperbacks—Seth M. Agnew, "God's Country & the Publisher," *Saturday Review,* 36 (March 14, 1953), 27. In 1959, eight of the top ten television series were Westerns—"Westerns: The Six-Gun Galahad," *Time,* 73 (March 30, 1959), 52.
13. Cawelti, *Adventure, Mystery, and Romance,* p. 193. See also Nye, *The Unembarrassed Muse,* pp. 300–302; and Jim Kitses, *Horizons West: Anthony Mann, Budd Boetticher, Sam Peckinpah: Studies of Authorship within the Western* (Bloomington, 1970), p. 11.
14. See Nye, *The Unembarrassed Muse,* p. 302.
15. See C. L. Sonnichsen, *From Hopalong to Hud: Thoughts on*

Western Fiction (College Station, Texas, and London, 1978), pp. 22–39, 157–75. Sickening! Don't miss it.

16. "Keeping Posted," *Saturday Evening Post*, 213 (March 15, 1941), 4.

17. Luke Short, "Ernest Haycox: An Appreciation," *Call Number*, 25 (Fall 1963–Spring 1964), 2–3.

18. Mrs. Eugene Manlove (May D.) Rhodes to Frederick D. Glidden, April 14, 1941; Ernest Haycox to Glidden, May 22, 1941—Frederick Dilley Glidden (Luke Short) Papers, University of Oregon Library, Eugene, Oregon. All letters to and from Glidden subsequently cited are in this collection.

19. Paul Trachtman, *The Gunfighters* (New York, 1974), pp. 35, 37; and Gary L. Roberts, "Short, Luke L.," pp. 1106–1107, in *The Reader's Encyclopedia of the American West*.

20. It has been said that Marguerite E. Harper, Glidden's New York literary agent from 1934 until her death in 1966, chose the name for him and that only later they learned who the real Luke Short had been. See "Luke Short Dies at 67: Was Long a Member of WWA [Western Writers of America]," *Roundup*, October 1975, p. 10. But the Glidden-Harper correspondence casts some doubt on this account. On March 22, 1935, he wrote her that he had signed "Luke Short" to his first book *(Single Shot Loot*, later called *The Feud at Single Shot)*, which he had just sent to her, but then invited her to make up a better name if she could. On April 20, 1935, she suggested that they use his real name for slicks and books, and Luke Short for pulps. On April 26, 1935, he signed another story Lew Short.

21. Sue Buck, " 'Luke Short'—Kewanee Boy Who Made Good," *Kewanee Star-Courier*, August 21, 1975, p. 3.

22. Office of Public Information, University of Missouri, April 24, 1957. Glidden worked for only three days for the *Minneapolis Star-Journal*. He and three partners pooled $200, went to northern Alberta, in Canada, and trapped fox, mink, and muskrat for two years, covering a 250-mile trapline with thirty-five dogs. The venture was an invigorating failure. H. Ray Baker, "The Short of It," *Denver Post* ("Rocky Mountain Empire Magazine" section), September 26, 1948, p. 8.

23. Idem; "Author of Westerns Fred Glidden Dies," *Aspen Times*, August 21, 1975, p. 16-A.

24. Harper to Glidden, December 28, 1937, January 3, 1939, January 2, 1940.

25. Glidden to Harper, January 11, February 25, June 15, 1938, and undated letter from England. Short tried to capitalize on the freighter voyage by writing a poor sea story based on conversations with the captain. See Steve Frazee, "Meet Fred Glidden," *Roundup*, October 1955, p. 3.

26. Harper to Glidden, October 16, 1940.

27. William K. Everson, in *A Pictorial History of the Western Film* (New York, 1969), calls the script "intelligently written," p. 188. See also Ernest N. Corneau, *The Hall of Fame of Western Film Stars* (North Quincy, Mass., 1969), p. 155.

28. Everson, in *A Pictorial History,* calls *Blood on the Moon* "one of the best scripted Westerns of the forties," p. 184. T.V. Olsen wrote me (July 23, 1979) that the originally assigned screenwriter's "script was so appalling that Short was forced to exercise his contractual option of script approval—and in this case, rewrote the entire script himself."

29. *Vengeance Valley* and *Ride the Man Down* became movies (same titles), while *High Vermilion* became the movie *Silver City.* Short's somewhat weaker novel *Ambush* also became a movie (same title).

30. Glidden to Harper, July 15, 1941.

31. A word about Short and money. The *Post* paid $10,000 for serial rights to *Ramrod* early in the 1940s, and $20,000 to *Vengeance Valley* late in the same decade. *Ramrod's* movie rights brought $25,000 more. Harper to Glidden, November 25, 1942, May 17, 1947, June 3, 1949. By contrast, Macmillan's 1945 hardbound edition of *And the Wind Blows Free* sold only 8,005 copies its first fifteen months and under four hundred more the next twelve months—sales statement from Macmillan, July 29, 1946 (1946 Harper-Glidden file); Harper to Glidden, August 4, 1947. *And the Wind Blows Free* was probably Short's best hardbound seller, with *Station West* and *Coroner Creek* following— sales statement from Houghton Mifflin, September 30, 1947 (1947 Harper-Glidden file); Harper to Glidden, August 4, September 3, 1947, June 1, 1948. Short received between 17.5 cents and 27 cents a copy on sales of these moderately priced hardbounds. Sales statements cited above. By contrast, in the late 1960s, Bantam guaranteed Short a minimum of $15,000 a year for an original paperback novel a year. Harper to Glidden, October 24, 1964. Short subsequently expressed his hope, fortunately a vain one, to do six such books in three years for a minimum of $90,000 from Bantam—Glidden to Harper, November 11, 1967. For a brief summary of this aspect of Short's career, see Etulain, "Development of the Western," p. 81.

32. *The Whip,* rejected by the *Post* (Harper to Glidden, August 16, 1956), was the first novel by Short to win an award, that of the second annual Maggie, Medallion of Merit. Oddly, when Short started *The Whip,* he gave the hero, in the first sentence, the name Dan Borthen, evidently forgetting that the hero of his *Rimrock,* his immediately earlier novel, was Dave Borthen, so named in the first sentence of that novel. Typescript of *The Whip,* Glidden Papers.

33. Harper to Glidden, February 14, March 18, 1950; Glidden to Harper, December 15, 1952.

34. For $20,000. As a condition of the sale of *Play a Lone Hand,* *Collier's* required that Short give them an option on his next novel.

Harper to Glidden, August 30, 1950. *Collier's* had already published four of Short's short stories.

35. Harper to Glidden, February 7 and 20, 1951.

36. Glidden to Harper, August 4, 1952. A copy of the musical comedy, together with playbills and local reviews, is in the Glidden Papers.

37. Glidden to Harper, August 4, September 30, October 27, 1952, November 18, 1955; Harper to Glidden, October 2, 1952; British lawyers to Harper, December 1, 1952; Dwight Newton to Robert L. Gale, July 31, 1979.

38. The *Post* accepted *Rimrock* for 1955 publication; it was the first Short serial to make it in the *Post* since *Vengeance Valley* (1949).

39. Harper to Bantam, June 21, 1955.

40. Glidden to Harper, September 6, 1955. Three years later, still interested in writing about aviation, Short hitched a ride on a NORAD bomber which then hurtled over Aspen for his amusement. He said that he was thinking of doing a novel on the Air Force with a China connection. Glidden to Harper, September 4, 1958. Billed as a public-relations stunt, this flight consumed $1,200 in jet fuel.

41. In the Glidden papers are four published teleplays by Short, all produced by the "Zane Grey Theater," in addition to several other such plays in various stages of completion. Steve Frazee, in "Meet Fred Glidden," p. 4, quotes Short as lamenting that he wasted too much time in Hollywood. See also "Luke Short Again Whacking the Keys," *Roundup*, August 1971, p. 16.

42. This story had been rejected by the *Saturday Evening Post*—*Post* to Harper, March 12, 1956; Harper to Glidden, April 13, 1956.

43. Harper to Glidden, June 17, 1958.

44. His opposition to myopic and greedy politicians at the town and country level is dramatized through a fictional screen in *Silver Rock* and also the unpublished novel *Pearley*. When citizens of Aspen thought that they could see resemblances between crooked council-men in *Silver Rock* and certain local officials, Short only smiled and admitted nothing. See "Luke Short Again Whacking the Keys," p. 8.

45. Eerily, Short wrote this soul-piercing lament just before, not just after, the tragic event. The original typescript of *First Claim*, which Short sent to his agent in April 1959, contains the generalization just quoted (Glidden Papers). When the *Saturday Evening Post* rejected it, the agent sold it at once to the *New York Daily* and *Sunday News*—Glidden to Harper, April 21, 1959; Harper to Glidden, May 29, 1959. So life followed art yet again.

46. Harper to Recife publisher, March 26, 1962.

47. Short later used in *The Stalkers* an incident from *Pearley* in which a prostitute walks down Main Street, nude, gun in hand, on a bet. In the published novel, the woman is named Pearl.

48. It promised 6 percent of list on sales to 500,000 copies, and 10 percent thereafter—Harper to Glidden, July 1, 1963. Meanwhile, Dell continued to reward Short valiantly for reprint rights to several of his earlier, less distinguished novels.

49. "Aspen—A View from a High Window," unpublished essay, Glidden Papers.

50. He wrote in detail of this projected sequence to both of his agents—Glidden to Harper, February 15, 1964, and Glidden to H.N. Swanson, February 15, 1964.

51. "Aspen—A View from a High Window."

Chapter Two

1. Shamrock is the first of several Short heroes who are modifications of the dime-novel outlaw hero, once highly popular; see Jones, *The Dime Novel Western*, pp. 76-88. Short called such heroes in his fiction Robin Hood types, not credible but entertaining—Glidden to Harper, April 2, 1953. T.V. Olsen opined in a letter to me (August 6, 1979) that such Short heroes are "strictly from comic-book country" but highly enjoyable.

2. Senator "Warrenrode" is mentioned in the later novel *Play a Lone Hand* (p. 74) as a land manipulator.

3. Note resemblances in place and person names to those in Walter Van Tilburg Clark's *Ox-Bow Incident*, published a year after Short's *Raiders of the Rimrock*.

4. Short wrote it in thirty days, and it remained one of his agent Miss Harper's favorites—Harper to Glidden, March 26, 1944, February 7, 1952.

5. See the laudatory review of it by G.W. Harris, in "New Western Tales," *New York Times Book Review*, February 9, 1941, p. 24.

6. Unbelievably, this minor rewriting was done in the editorial office without Short's knowledge. Short was amused, since the Canada of the original story was based on his 1930s experiences there; but he was unprofessionally indifferent, too—Glidden to Harper, April 3, 1961.

7. The complex plot made *Raw Land* a best-selling Dell comic book when it was published as *Six Gun Ranch* in 1954.

8. By late 1962 the Bantam reprint of *Gunman's Chance* had sold 803,300 copies and was then one of Short's five top best-sellers. The others were *Ride the Man Down* (1,403,000 copies), *Coroner Creek* (996,100). *Hardcase* (874,600), and *Sunset Graze* (810,200). Harper to Bantam, May 13, 1963; Bantam to Harper, May 24, 1963; [Harper] to Glidden, August 1, 1963.

9. *Deadline* was Short's working title—Harper to Glidden, December 19, 1940.

10. They are Andrew Johnson, Chester Arthur, Grover Cleveland, Henry M. Teller, L.Q.C. Lamar, William T. Sherman, and Philip H. Sheridan. Incidentally, *Desert Crossing* names John Pope and Jim Bowie.

11. James K. Folsom, in *The American Western Novel* (New Haven, 1966), singles out only this novel by Short for praise, calling it "a more successful Western detective story than [Max Brand's] *Destry Rides Again*" (p. 114).

12. Phillip D. Thomas, in "The Paperback West of Luke Short," *Journal of Popular Culture*, 7 (Winter 1973), 702-704, singles out the town of Vermilion here as a typical one in Short's fiction.

13. An even lovelier phrase is "naked to the starlight" from the earlier *Sunset Graze* (p. 115).

14. In a letter (Glidden to Harper, November 16, 1953), Short identifies the locale as Colorado but does not do so in the novel itself.

15. Here Short is probably not so much following the gory example of Owen Wister's *Virginian* as he is that of several dime novels of an earlier era. See Jones, *The Dime Novel Western*, pp. 104, 108-109.

16. The *Saturday Evening Post* injudiciously rejected *Desert Crossing* because it had too many scene shifts—Harper to Glidden, October 13, 1960. In reality, the changes are handled with great skill.

17. Short had considerable trouble writing this novel. The following bothered him: the Colorado background, the marital status of the sheriff, the pseudodramatics of his wife, and the disappearance of Minnie Gerba's corpse—Glidden to Harper, November 21, 1960, February 28, August 15, September 20, December 13, 1961.

18. Short also saw the connection between his Primrose and Faulkner's "Yaknapatapha [*sic*]"—Glidden to Harper, May 4, 1965.

19. Selby is named Louis Selby in *The Primrose Try*, Short's second Primrose novel. Short devoted much thought to Primrose, which he regarded as his most nearly perfect fictional background (Glidden to Harper, December 16, 1964), and for which he had elaborate street plans and building floor plans and elevation plans drawn (Glidden Papers).

20. Helping Tish to decide on the hero was to have been her rape, or a threat thereof, by the villain.

21. Her last name, Frost, appears too soon after that of the virtuous heroine of *Desert Crossing*—Juliana Frost. Short refused to cut *First Campaign*, which is unusually long and which he called "epic"— Glidden to Harper, [March 15, 1964], March 24, 1965.

22. The political situation which forms the background of *The Outrider* is based upon an incident in Colorado politics. See "Luke Short Again Whacking the Keys," p. 8.

23. Upon rereading the novel, we can see that this "surprise" has been quietly prepared for.

Chapter Three

1. See *The Sound of Mountain Water* (New York, 1969.

2. In *Debt of Honor,* "the restless West" is described as full of wanderers (p. 22).

3. One of the most devastatingly icy winters in Western history occurred in 1885-86. See Ernest Staples Osgood, *The Day of the Cattleman* (Minneapolis, 1929; rpt. Chicago and London, n.d.), pp. 216-22.

4. Half of Short's ranches are built near soothing cottonwoods. In *Raw Land,* "a single tall cottonwood [is] an eye-hurting emerald-green against the red hills" (p. 126).

5. See Cawelti, *Adventure, Mystery, and Romance,* pp. 242-43.

6. The reader hopes in vain that something vital will be made of the beautiful, wind-chopped lake near the Triangle H in *Donovan's Gun.*

7. See also *The Primrose Try,* pp. 9, 116.

8. According to Jones, *The Dime Western Novel,* "the unlimited openness of the western landscape is perhaps the most functional aspect of the Western's setting. . ." (p. 129).

9. Short points out here and elsewhere that foreign-born laborers really won the West—for the WASPs. For confirmation, see Frank Bergon and Zeese Papanikolas, eds., *Looking Far West: The Search for the American West in History, Myth, and Literature* (New York and Scarborough, Ontario, 1978), pp. 6-7.

10. Moffat's return to town and his subsequent muddy fight make him feel, "for the first time in three years, washed clean of guilt" (p. 48). It almost seems that Short is saying that men can gash Mother Nature to gory mud and be cleansed by the activity of it all, but that women should be more dainty and passive.

11. Ranches can be too feminized, however. See Mrs. Harms's ranch, nicknamed the Henhouse, in *Coroner Creek,* and Bucksaw, the spread owned by Sophie's domineering, prissy mother, Maud Barrick, in *The Guns of Hanging Lake.*

12. Short offers a remarkable tour of a typically grand ranch house when he has Varney, the bastard in *First Campaign,* stride through his father's Big House and take a ritual drink in each room. The result is prolonged intoxication.

13. Often, in a fancy courthouse, the second floor is given over to the Masonic lodge. But no Masonic meetings occur in any Short novel.

14. The play *The Front Page* by Ben Hecht and Charles MacArthur

(1928) features a somewhat similar escape that may have inspired Short's 1936 rendition.

Chapter Four

1. There is only one little girl in Short. She is Lydia Beale *(Saddle by Starlight)*, who hero-worships her widowed mother's foreman, Sam Holley, and once adoringly makes him a repulsive sandwich, which he considerately accepts only to discard it quietly in the forest.

2. *The Americans: The Democratic Experience*, p. 34.

3. Arrogance is usually a virtue in Short's fiction.

4. Coyle's analysis of the rich man is reminiscent of that of F. Scott Fitzgerald, in "Rich Boy" (1926): "They possess and enjoy early, and it does something to them, makes them soft where we are hard, and cynical where we are trustful. . ."

5. Reading Chapter 10, entitled "Lying to Enemies" (pp. 134-45), in Sissela Bok's *Lying: Moral Choice in Public and Private Life* (New York, 1978), would make Reeves smile. He would then explain that by lies he could defeat his enemy, who would then realize too late that he should have expected no less. Reeves persuades Beth Fanning to participate in his scheme of subterfuge. Eastern though she is, he loses no respect in her eyes; after all, according to the Western code, he is the man and hence knows best.

6. *Anatomy of Criticism: Four Essays* (Princeton, 1957), p. 366.

7. This sequence in mysteries is mathematically spaced: see Chapters 7, 10, 11, and 14.

8. Sam Kinsley *(Sunset Graze)* and Ben Judd *(Three for the Money)*, both lawmen, are also sexual rivals of the heroes of the respective novels and yet, in different ways, also aid those heroes professionally. Mead Calhan *(Vengeance Valley)*, Sam Avery *(Summer of the Smoke)*, and Benjy Schell *(The Guns of Hanging Lake)*, though not lawmen, are also sexual rivals of the heroes but do not let this competition keep them from acting with manly responsibility.

9. It is of interest that the first mention of the sheriff in *High Vermilion* comes in the last chapter.

10. A repulsive habit which marks this villain, as well as a few others in Short, is that of cutting his chewing tobacco and then carefully licking the knife before repocketing it. Orville Hoad, arch villain of *Paper Sheriff*, sets his half-chewed cud on the table when he eats, then resumes the cud.

11. This type also includes Warner Sands *(Raiders of the Rimrock)*, Lieutenant Benson *(Summer of the Smoke)*, Lieutenant Joshua Miller *(Desert Crossing)*, and Lew Seely *(The Man from Two Rivers)*.

12. The eyes of Sheriff Wes Canning *(Man from the Desert)* would seem to foreshadow similar uncontrollable villainy: "A blocky man of

thirty stepped in, nodded curtly. . .and laid a cold glance on Hanaway. His eyes were of the palest amber and he couldn't have hid [*sic*] the wildness in them if he'd tried, which he didn't" (p. 12). But Canning, in spite of subsequent bluster, turns inexplicably passive, in a nice touch by Short.

13. Albie Meacham's name seems unimaginatively close to that of Short's earlier villain Albie Beecham of *Fiddlefoot*.

14. Crippled fathers of attractive heroines are a rather frequent character type in Western dime novels. See Jones, *The Dime Novel Western*, pp. 154, 158.

15. Full-bosomed women are featured with never-monotonous regularity in Short, who, however, has Tully Gibbs *(Silver Rock)* rather crudely note to himself after his first close view that Sarah Moffit was "slim, long-legged, just top-heavy enough, and with a beautiful face" (p. 23).

Chapter Five

1. Trans, Lucille Ray (Boston, 1916; rpt. 1968).

2. *The Pulp Jungle* (Los Angeles, 1967), pp. 184–86.

3. See *Six Guns and Society: A Structural Study of the Western* (Berkeley, Los Angeles, and London, 1975), pp. 29–123 passim.

4. In fairness to Short, it should be repeated that, when he sought to break out of his formulaic straitjacket, he was discouraged by his agent and sometimes rejected by his regular publishers.

5. E. Allen Tilley would categorize all of Short's novels as examples of the Romance, with many in "The Swift Kick" group, some in "The Hero as Breakfast Food" group, a few in "The Masked Stranger" group, and many in "The Final Confrontation" group. See his "The Modes of Fiction: A Plot Morphology," *College English*, 39 (February 1978), 695–96.

6. Edna Johnson et al., eds., *Anthology of Children's Literature*, 5th ed. (Boston, 1977), p. 288. Short has the apparent heroine of *Fiddlefoot*, early in the novel (p. 14), hold off the hero until he proves that he is "the Young Prince" and she "the Princess," and that he deserves "to live happily ever after" with her. Later they split up. It almost seems that Short builds plot out of certain fairy-tale ingredients but wants his characters to feel realistically motivated.

7. (New York, 1949; Cleveland and New York, 1956). Quotations will be cited parenthetically in the text and are from the later edition.

8. I take note of Walter Sutton's warning against mechanically applying Campbell's useful insights. See *Modern American Criticism* (Englewood Cliffs, N.J., 1963), pp. 181–82.

9. Aristotle would approve of Short more than E. M. Forster would. See his *Aspects of the Novel* (New York, 1927, 1954), pp. 83–86.

10. But once he is personally affronted, he acts decisively, saying that "he. . .would not turn the other cheek" (p. 102). As Sissela Bok says in her chapter entitled "Lying to Enemies," "The idea that one should turn the other cheek to an enemy is profoundly alien to. . .intuitive morality" (*Lying*, p. 136).

11. He appears almost like an answer to Jack Cope's sibyllic prediction, according to Mary, who says, " 'Years ago Uncle Jack told me that there would come a time we were waiting for and a man we were waiting for. . . .You're the man, Jim Wade' " (pp. 61, 62).

12. Selena's action constitutes only a minor subplot, designed to complicate the essentially thin main plot. Short wrote his agent to the effect that he was stuck while writing *Last Hunt* until he hit on the idea of having the sheriff married; Short also saw Selena as not only ignorant but also ruined by a diet of TV soap operas—Glidden to Harper, September 20, 1961. *Vengeance Valley* has a similarly functional subplot when Lily Fasken seems tempting to young Martin Sambrook, Jr., who at the end behaves like a knight sent on a quest.

13. Short loved and was adept at this sport—Baker, "The Short of It," p. 8. See also *The Guns of Hanging Lake*, pp. 8–9.

14. Indeed, Short's initial plan for *Last Hunt* called for a story about a doctor who trailed his father's murderer—Glidden to Harper, November 21, 1960.

15. It is touching when seasoned old cowpokes and ranch owners address younger men as "son," as they frequently do in Short. See *The Feud at Single Shot*, p. 132; *Raiders of the Rimrock,* pp. 134, 139, 141, 142, 143; and *Gunman's Chance*, p. 200.

16. Pete Brisbin lies to account for his West Point educational polish thus: " 'I was a schoolteacher. . .in a men's prison' " (*The Deserters*, p. 20).

17. With a somewhat unsatisfactory assist from an inartistic novelist, who, some eight chapters later, without a pause in his stride, has Hal fortuitously reveal that " 'I've turned down an offer of thirty thousand for my [modest?] spread up north, thanks to old Jeff Kittrick [who made Hal his heir]' " (p. 160).

18. Two slatternly women are born survivors, stolidly helping no one but themselves. They are ex-prostitute Norah in *The Deserters* and Minnie, Orv Hoad's unspeaking Ute Indian wife in *Paper Sheriff.*

19. The reader is expected to endorse the implied message that Carrie will forget the multiple killings because they are now a thing of the past. More credible is Kate Shayne's gradual acceptance of Western ways, in *Bold Rider,* and the realistic change by Kate Hardison of her philosophy to conform to that of a hero whom she cannot help admiring, in *Coroner Creek.*

Chapter Six

1. "It would be too rash a generalization to say that every serious novel has some dominant theme; but it is often both possible and helpful to find one"; Marjorie Boulton, *The Anatomy of the Novel* (London and Boston, 1975), p. 141.

2. "I pay for what I break" was the motto of Eugene Manlove Rhodes, whom Short admired. For information on Rhodes, see W. H. Hutchinson, "I Pay for What I Break," *Western American Literature*, 1 (Summer 1966), 91–96.

3. Dell, which reprinted *Gunsmoke Graze* (1940) as *Raw Land* in January 1952, asked Short's permission to change the title of *Six Guns of San Jon* (1938) to a better follow-up title, *Savage Range*, for its August 1952 reprint—Harper to Glidden, March 13, 1952.

4. A glance at his bibliography will show that Short often had trouble with his titles. He frequently wrote to his agent to this effect, and often authorized her to try for a better title or let his publishers do so.

5. When the hero of *The Stalkers* grows a beard to disguise himself from the villain, the villain shaves off his beard so that the hero will less readily recognize him. After the hero lures the villain into town by jailing his accomplices, the villain lures the hero to his robbers' roost by kidnapping the hero's girl friend.

6. The ability of villains in Western fiction to subvert the processes of law and order is a common feature of innumerable dime novels. See Jones, *The Dime Novel Western*, pp. 122, 127.

7. For a good one, see *The Outrider*, pp. 135, 136, in which the hero regards himself as having no choice but to seek a killer's trail, which trail itself takes on the contours of a Hawthornean symbol of fate.

8. Interestingly, just a few pages later the hero lectures the heroine to the effect that " 'we give people a choice every day. If a man knows I carry money with me, he's got a choice. He can rob me or leave me alone. . . . Our whole life is a series of choices' " (p. 126).

9. Good men even respect the loyalty of villains' henchmen. For example, see *The Outrider*, p. 40.

10. He sounds a little like Herman Melville's Billy Budd, when that ill-starred fellow explains that he is loyal to the crown: " '. . .I have eaten the King's bread and I am true to the King.' "

11. Julia Rainey in *Saddle by Starlight* is seemingly disloyal, but only temporarily and only through ignorance. Lottie Priest in *Ride the Man Down* declines to remain loyal to the hero, informs against him, puts him in danger, and therefore loses him.

12. For an especially sad case, that of a woman who lets two men

think for her, see Kate Miles in *First Claim,* especially pp. 130–31, 136.

13. He even affectionately calls her "idiot girl," later, and tells her to stand up for a kiss (p. 126).

14. He somewhat resembles Huck Finn, who is willing to steal Jim out of slavery but loses his respect for Tom Sawyer when the latter offers to join him in the lowdown business.

15. Tender memories in these circumstances seem to be something almost hated in Short. See *The Deserters,* p. 68.

16. Most curiously, his vision at one point seems to be improving, but Short drops the matter and makes nothing thematic of it.

17. In a charming generalization, the villain in *Summer of the Smoke* opines that "it was the unnecessary lies that trapped a man" (p. 81).

18. Interestingly, in *Sunset Graze* the sheriff sides with the villain, who when tripped up tells more credible lies; yet the sheriff calls the truth-telling hero " 'a cabinet-piece liar' " (p. 81).

19. If Short's lying heroes (and villains, too, for that matter) could have read Sissela Bok's *Lying,* they would have responded positively to her statement that liars seek both to avoid harm and to produce benefits (pp. 78–81), would have known how to answer her rhetorical question: "If at times force can be used to counter force, why should lies never be used to counter lies?" (p. 126), and would have agreed totally with her brilliant analogy of life as "a game of poker. . . [which] mingles trust and distrust, bargaining and gambling" (p. 130).

Chapter Seven

1. The closest literary analogue to Short is Ernest Hemingway. Echoes or resemblances occur in at least the following: *Hard Money,* p. 101; *Dead Freight for Piute,* p. 146; *High Vermilion,* pp. 84, 144, 147; *The Whip,* p. 92; *First Campaign,* p. 54; *The Guns of Hanging Lake,* p. 101; *Three for the Money,* p. 119; *The Outrider,* p. 133; and *The Man from Two Rivers,* p. 100.

2. See also *Last Hunt,* pp. 95–96, and *The Primrose Try,* pp. 49–54. This feature is hardly surprising in view of Short's experience writing for Hollywood and the television industry. Short even has one curious movie simile: " '. . .it [the bachelor speaker's untidy room] always looks as if they just shot a cowboy movie in it an hour ago' " (*Silver Rock,* p. 36).

3. For other skillful scene shifts, see *Rimrock,* Chapter 5, and *Last Hunt,* Chapter 2. Short was cooperative with the editors of *Collier's* in making about thirty minor revisions in *Silver Rock* but refused to comply with one request, since, as he put it, to do so would inartistically violate the hero's point of view—Glidden to Harper, February 27, 1953.

4. Everything that Robie Macauley and George Lanning say about good dialogue in their *Technique in Fiction* (New York, Evanston, and London, 1964), pp. 51–56, reads like implicit praise of Short's techniques.

5. Forster, *Aspects of the Novel,* p. 67; Boulton, *The Anatomy of the Novel,* p. 81.

6. Forster, *Aspects of the Novel,* pp. 71, 68.

7. Oddly, the hero of Clay Fisher's 1958 novel *The Crossing* is named Jud Reeves. The villain in Short's 1967 *Debt of Honor* is Jud, and its hero is Reeves.

8. Tina's eyes are memorably described as green and then turn blue (pp. 2, 13).

9. Short almost makes it a habit to name several characters in a given work with identical initial sounds. Thus we have Beauchamp, Ben, Bonsell, and Buckner in *Savage Range;* Sarita, Seay, Sharon, Shore, and Stole in *Hard Money;* Cole, Cornwall, Craig, and Keen in *Dead Freight for Piute;* Celia, Sam, Santee, Shorty, and Steve in *Bought with a Gun;* and Cameron, Carpenter, Christina, Cross, Crowder, Curly, and Kimball, and even McCabe, in *Three for the Money.* Short's agent complained of this habit very early in their professional relationship (evidently to no avail)—Harper to Glidden, April 26, 1935.

10. Short replied to an inquisitive fan on May 13, 1966, that he had never written about ministers or about men dressed like ministers.

11. Rita, though attractive, is decent and passive and hence is an exception to the dime-novel stereotype of the "fiery and passionate woman of Latin blood" (Jones, *The Dime Novel Western,* p. 144).

12. See especially pp. 26, 41, 45, 79. Short also shows sympathy for Mexican Catholics by the same device of having disreputable WASPs make ridiculous remarks about them; see *Trouble Country,* pp. 90, 95, 128, 135. Two of the most abused women in all of Short appear in these two novels.

13. He did not think so and wrote to that effect to his agent— Glidden to Harper, June 25, 1958; see also Harper to Glidden, May 6, 1957. But many friends attest to his sense of humor.

14. It may be only accidental, but most of the above examples of humor occur in the first half of the novels from which they are taken. Perhaps Short felt that humor would not mix well with his habitually murderous climaxes.

15. Short gives titles to chapters in only four novels, none after *Raw Land.*

16. Short also puns on Will Ferrin's name in *Saddle by Starlight:* "Through an iron effort of will Ferrin would not let himself think. . ." (p. 53).

17. *Three for the Money,* in spite of frightening violence, is also lightened by occasional comic dialogue; see, for example, pp. 80, 98. A

mounted moose head in *Barren Land Showdown* is described as knocked off the wall during a fight and then appearing to sniff in unblinking alarm at a crack in the floor (pp. 118-19).

18. The reader would not do too badly if he also read Laurence Ivan Seidman, *Once in the Saddle: The Cowboy's Frontier 1866-1896* (New York 1973; rpt. New York and Scarborough, Ontario, 1973). Bergon and Papanikolas date the cowboy era 1865-87, in their superb anthology, *Looking Far West*, p. 242.

19. The heroine of *Silver Rock* teaches Sunday school but plays hookey from the sermon one day after her class. The hero of *The Outrider* attends a church funeral, but no details are provided other than mention of the smell of the miners who are there to mourn. One woman is a devout Catholic but is depicted as too passive to warrant Short's presenting aspects of her faith *(Trouble Country)*. Another woman is an unpleasant schoolteacher, but she is shown only once in her schoolhouse and then after the pupils have left for home *(Ride the Man Down)*.

20. See particularly *Fiddlefoot*, Chapters 9, 11, 13. Most surprisingly, Short did not like horses; see Baker, "The Short of It," p. 8.

21. This may be an appropriate place to mention that the writers of the material on Short's paperback covers and in the pretextual "previews" contribute to the reverse of verisimilitude. The back cover of Bantam's *Hard Money* reprint identifies the locale of the action as Nevada, which is not specified in the text. The preview material of Bantam's 1959 *Silver Rock* reprint tells of hero Tully Gibbs's being pinned down by rifle fire and having "his own gun a deadly three yards away from his hand," but not so in the text. The back cover of Bantam's 1968 *Donovan's Gun* identifies deceased old Burt Hethridge as Cole, whereas Cole is Burt's son and is very much alive through much of the novel. Moreover, several posttextual biographical blurbs, including some of Dell's as well as Bantam's, incorrectly give Short's birth year as 1907. Short tried to do his part to improve the often shoddy covers of Western paperbacks. See Fred Glidden, "What Editors Want in Western Covers," *Roundup*, December 1955, pp. 3-5.

Chapter Eight

1. It is also revealing that the working title of *Donovan's Gun* was *Donovan's Week*—Glidden papers.

2. Among the Glidden papers is a carefully written fourteen-page outline for a motion-picture adaptation of *Three for the Money*, which indicates that as late in the early 1970s Short entertained hopes for a Hollywood comeback.

3. Curiously, less action is specified on Sundays in Short's novels

than on other days. In fact, in *Debt of Honor* the hero and heroine would appear to lose an entire Sunday (see pp. 85, 90), although the villainous newspaper editor is busy breaking the Sabbath nefariously.

4. Working notes on *Trouble Country* in the Glidden papers concern locale—Rocky Mountain Central mountains—but not time sequences.

5. See also *Donovan's Gun*, pp. 124, 126, 127, in which Donovan hears from his place in the cemetery the distant gunfire which we already know is sweeping Cole Hethridge, Keefe Hart, and others to their death.

6. A similar stylistic trick is Short's having his characters pause in their talk for the purpose of rhetorical emphasis. See *King Colt*, p. 185; *The Guns of Hanging Lake*, pp. 19-20, 54; *Man from the Desert*, p. 52.

7. Contributing to verisimilitude and the unity of time is Short's occasional indication of the year or years during which action in certain novels occurs: *Station West*, 1872; *Dead Freight for Piute*, 1873; *Coroner Creek* and *First Claim*, 1879; *First Campaign*, 1882; *Play a Lone Hand*, *The Some-Day Country*, and *The Man from Two Rivers*, 1883; *And the Wind Blows Free*, 1884-85; *The Feud at Single Shot*, after 1893; and *The Man on the Blue*, before 1896. The last two dates may be inferred from hints as to statehood. Four Short novels take place during or slightly later than the era of the Korean War: *Barren Land Showdown*, *Silver Rock*, *Rimrock*, and *Last Hunt*. Action in the rest of Short's works occurs between 1866 and 1896, in all probability, during the heyday of the cowpuncher. Miss Harper asked Short to pinpoint the date of action in *Ride the Man Down*, to help the *Saturday Evening Post* illustrator; she guessed it was the 1880s—Harper to Glidden, January 5, 1942.

8. The specific state is unidentifiable. One contemporary reviewer thought it was Arizona; another, Colorado. As for the locale of *Play a Lone Hand*, reviewers located it in Arizona, Nevada, and New Mexico. Clipping file, Glidden Papers.

9. His agent complained to Short that he overused the word "Stetson"—Harper to Glidden, February 22, 1943. In his early works, he certainly does.

10. Quoted in Macauley and Lanning, *Technique in Fiction*, p. 39.

11. The letters exchanged between Short and his agent are often very sloppy, but they got the job done. It should be added that the Dell paperback reprints and the Bantam paperback reprints and originals of Short's novels have dozens of punctuation errors, spelling errors, and typos; but Short is less to be blamed for these than his slipshod editors.

12. Cam is wise. Early kisses are rare in Short and usually do not pay off in later bliss. Kisses midway through a given novel are often remembered uneasily, even with guilt. Short is almost as Victorian as William Dean Howells in this regard. See Kenneth Eble, "Howells'

Kisses," *American Quarterly*, 9 (Winter 1957), 441–47.

13. More graphic is "one great mushroom of pain before blackness," in *Ambush*, p. 90.

14. One tough man prefers to be called " 'Mr. son of a bitch' " (*The Stalkers*, p. 91), rather than simply "son of a bitch," which strikes him as familiar.

15. As explained in Chapter 1, Short published these harrowing lines in 1960, the year in which his older son James accidentally drowned.

16. See also *Ambush*, pp. 17–18, 124; *The Guns of Hanging Lake*, p. 16.

17. His agent once wrote Short that he had just the proper amount of cynicism to qualify him to write the Great American Novel—Harper to Glidden, May 21, 1945.

Chapter Nine

1. Harper to Glidden, March 4, 1940.

2. Harper to Glidden, January 29, 1958.

3. Harper to Glidden, January 30, 1953.

4. Glidden to Harper, May 16, 1938.

5. Glidden to Harper, March 15, 1964.

6. Glidden to Harper, April 1, 1957. Short originally called the story "The Drowned Emma."

7. Brian Garfield, "The Fiddlefoot from Kewanee," *Roundup*, November 1975, 6–7, 11; Bantam to Glidden, July 15, 1958.

8. Luke Short, "Foreword," p. v. in *Bad Men and Good: A Roundup of Western Stories by Members of the Western Writers of America* (New York, 1953). Steve Frazee wrote me (July 25, 1979) as follows: "One of Glidden's favorite remarks was that Western writers should not be angrily exercised over the fact that their work was not accorded the status of great novels. 'We are,' he said, 'honorable entertainers who need apologize to no one.' "

9. Glidden to Harper, May 13, 1966.

Selected Bibliography

PRIMARY SOURCES

NOTE: Key to dates used: following "s," year of serial publication or year such publication started; following "hb," first hardbound book publication; "pb," first paperback book publication. Titles in parentheses are alternates used in publications specified by abbreviations and dates given. Facts of publication which then follow are for paperbacks cited in the present study. Page numbers of Luke Short's novels referred to in the text are from paperback editions by Bantam Books, Dell Publishing Company, and Fawcett Publications.

1. Novels (Complete, Chronological)
The Feud at Single Shot; s 1935, hb 1936, pb 1950. New York: Bantam, 1950.
The Branded Man; s 1936 *(Rustler's Range),* hb 1939 *(Weary Range),* pb 1956. New York: Dell, 1966.
The Man on the Blue; s 1936, hb 1937 *(Guns of the Double Diamond),* pb 1954. New York: Dell, 1975.
Marauders' Moon; s 1937 *(Silver Horn Breaks),* hb 1938 *(Bull-Foot Ambush),* pb 1955. New York: Dell, 1955.
King Colt; s 1937, pb 1953. New York: Dell, 1957.
Brand of Empire; s 1937 *(Red Trail to Black Treasure),* hb 1940, pb 1959. New York: Dell, 1977.
Bold Rider; s 1938 *(Gun-Hammered Gold),* hb 1939 *(The Gold Rustlers),* pb 1953. New York: Dell, 1975.
Savage Range; s 1938 *(Trouble Fighter),* hb 1939 *(Six Guns of San Jon),* pb 1952. New York: Dell, 1976.
Raiders of the Rimrock; s 1938 *(Death Rides Tornado Basin),* hb 1939, pb 1949. New York: Bantam, 1957.
Hard Money; s 1938 *(Golden Acres),* hb 1939 *(Flood Water),* pb 1949. New York: Dell, 1959.
Bounty Guns; s 1939, hb 1940, pb 1953. New York: Dell, 1976.
War on the Cimarron; s 1939 *(Hurricane Range),* hb 1940, pb 1950. New York: Bantam, 1959.
Dead Freight for Piute; s 1939, hb 1940, hb 1941 *(Western Freight),* pb 1950 *(Bull Whip).* New York: Bantam, 1957.
Bought with a Gun; s 1940 *(Gun Bought Grant),* hb 1943, pb 1955. New York: Dell, 1955.

171

Barren Land Showdown; s 1940 *(Spy of the North),* pb 1951*(Barren Land Murders).* Greenwich, Conn.: Fawcett, 1957.

Raw Land; s 1940 *(Gunsmoke Graze),* hb 1944 *(Gauntlet of Fire),* pb 1952. New York: Dell, 1977.

Gunman's Chance; s 1941 *(Blood on the Moon),* hb 1941, pb 1948 *(Blood on the Moon),* pb 1956. New York: Bantam, 1976.

Hardcase; s 1941, hb 1942, pb 1947. New York: Bantam, 1955.

Ride the Man Down; s 1942, hb 1942, pb 1947. New York: Bantam, 1961.

Sunset Graze; hb 1942, pb 1949 *(The Rustlers).* New York: Bantam, 1956.

And the Wind Blows Free; s 1943, hb 1945, pb 1950. New York: Bantam, 1955.

Ramrod; s 1943, hb 1943, pb 1960. New York: Bantam, 1977.

Coroner Creek; s 1945, hb 1946, pb 1948. New York: Bantam, 1956.

Fiddlefoot; s 1946, hb 1949, pb 1951. New York: Bantam, 1956.

Station West; s 1946, hb 1947, pb 1948. New York: Bantam, 1976.

High Vermilion; s 1947, hb 1948, pb 1949 *(Hands Off!).* New York: Bantam, 1956.

Vengeance Valley; s 1949, hb 1950, pb 1951. New York: Bantam, 1972.

Ambush; s 1948, hb 1950, pb 1951. New York: Bantam, 1958.

Play a Lone Hand; s 1950, hb 1951, pb 1953. New York: Bantam, 1974.

Saddle by Starlight; s 1952, hb 1952, pb 1959. New York: Bantam, 1959.

Silver Rock; s 1953, hb 1953, pb 1959. New York: Bantam, 1959.

Rimrock; s 1955 *(Fool's Treasure),* hb 1955, pb 1954. New York: Bantam, 1974.

The Whip; s 1956 *(Doom Cliff),* pb 1957, hb 1958. New York: Bantam, 1957.

Summer of the Smoke; pb 1958, hb 1959. New York: Bantam, 1958.

First Claim; s 1960, pb 1960, hb 1961. New York: Bantam, 1960.

Desert Crossing; s 1961, pb 1961, hb 1963. New York: Bantam, 1961.

Last Hunt; s 1962, pb 1962, hb 1963. New York: Bantam, 1962.

The Some-Day Country; s 1963, pb 1964, hb 1965 *(Trigger Country).* New York: Bantam, 1964.

First Campaign; pb 1965. New York: Bantam, 1973.

Paper Sheriff; s 1965, pb 1966. New York: Bantam, 1966.

The Primrose Try; s 1966, pb 1967. New York: Bantam, 1967.

Debt of Honor; pb 1967. New York: Bantam, 1967.

The Guns of Hanging Lake; s 1968, pb 1968. New York: Bantam, 1968.

Donovan's Gun; pb 1968. New York: Bantam, 1968.

The Deserters; pb 1969. New York: Bantam, 1969.

Three for the Money; pb 1970. New York: Bantam, 1970.

Man from the Desert; pb 1971. New York: Bantam, 1971.

The Outrider; pb 1972. New York: Bantam, 1972.

The Stalkers; pb 1973. New York: Bantam, 1973.
The Man from Two Rivers; pb 1974. New York: Bantam, 1974.
Trouble Country; pb 1976. New York: Bantam, 1976.

2. Short Stories
Only selected stories arranged by magazine and newspaper are included, to show Short's range in pulp and slick publication. Bibliographical data are incomplete to save space. Dates indicate month and year of publication in monthly magazines (or month in which serials started), and month and year only, not day as well, in which other stories were published in nonbook form. A couple of stories appearing in anthologies are added.

Ace-High Magazine: "Doc Potter's Six-Gun Cure" (9/36), "Death Cold-Decks a Tinhorn" (11/37).
Ace-High Western: "Fighting Nesters of Sacaton" (11/36).
Adventure: "Sun of a Gun-Curse" (4/36), "Hideout" (8/39), "The Fence" (3/40), "Exile" (8/41).
All-American Fiction: "Roll, Jordan" (12/37).
Argosy: "Tough Enough" (9/37), "Lobo Quarantine" (6/38), "Light the War Fires" (9/38), "First Judgment" (10/38), "Indian Scare" (3/39), "Some Dogs Steal" (6/39), "Brassguts" (7/41), "Paper Hero" (9/41), "Bitter Frontier" (4/42), "Trumpets West" (7/45; New York: Dell, 1957).
Big-Book Western: "Bandit Lawman" (3/37).
Blue Book: "The Ivory Butt Plate" (8/37), "The Right Kind of Tough" (10/37), "Rough Shod" (4/39), "The Strange Affair at Seven Troughs" (6/41), "Neutral Spirits" (1/42).
Chicago Tribune: "Finish the Fable" (3/41), "Feel My Muscle" (9/41).
Collier's: "The Warning" (1/38), "Court Day" (5/39), "Belabor Day" (9/39), "The Doctor Keeps a Promise" (3/40).
Country Home: "Brand of Justice" (2/39).
Cowboy Stories: "Six-Gun Lawyer" (8/35), "Bounty Hunter" (11/35), "Long Rider Lawman" (6/36), "Trial by Fury" (9/36).
Denver Post: "Make Mine Dark" (3/39).
Detective Story: "White Horse, Black Horse" (1/42), "Second-Guesser" (5/42).
Dime Adventure Magazine: "Gambler's Glory" (12/35), "Border Rider" (1/36).
Dime Western Magazine: "Gun-Boss of Broken Men" (4/36), "Buckskin Popper's Last Ride" (1/37), "Town-Tamer on the Dodge" (4/37), "The Marshal of Vengeance" (7/37).
Dynamic Adventures: "Caribou Copper" (10/35), "Walker" (3/36).
The Fall Roundup, ed. Harry E. Maule (New York: Random House, 1955): "The Drummer."

Iron Men and Silver Stars, ed. Donald Hamilton (Greenwich, Conn.:
Fawcett, 1967): "The Hangman" (substantially revised from "Pull
Your Freight!"—see *Riders West* below).
Liberty: "Snipes Til June" (10/40).
New York Sunday News: "Holy Show" (8/40), "The Teehanner" (1/42),
"Bad Exit" (10/44).
Riders West (New York: Dell, 1956): "Pull Your Freight!" (substan-
tially revised as "The Hangman"—see *Iron Men and Silver Stars*
above).
Saturday Evening Post: "Top Hand" (10/43), "The Danger Hole" (8/
48).
Short Stories: "A Mistake in Crates" (5/40), "Countermand" (7/40),
"Smuggler's Berg" (9/40).
Ski Magazine: "Does a Spectre Haunt Our Skiing?" (12/51).
Star Western: "Gamblers Don't Quit" (10/35), "Blood of His Enemies"
(10/35), "Gun Boss of Hell's Wells" (12/35), "Guns for a
Peacemaker" (2/36), "Tinhorn's Last Gamble" (4/36), "Outlaws
Make Good Neighbors" (10/36), "The Buzzard Basin Gun Stam-
pede" (11/36), "Buckshot Freighter" (12/36), "The Ghost Deputy
of Doubletree" (6/37).
Ten Story Western: "Boothill Ride" (8/36), "Boothill Brotherhood"
(10/36), "War Fires Light the Stage Trails" (2/38).
This Week: "Hurry, Charlie, Hurry" (8/40), "Ten O'clock Spot" (8/41).
Thrilling Western Stories: "Gunslick Gold" (3/37).
Top-Notch: "Booze-Head Heritage" (7/36).
Western Story: "Payoff at Rain Peak" (4/38), "Test Pit" (1/39; New
York: Dell, 1958—*Top Gun*), "Swindle in Piute Sink" (5/39),
"Lead Won't Lie" (9/39).
Western Trails: "Gunhawks Die Hard" (11/36).

3.   Criticism (Chronological)
"Foreword," pp. v–vii, to *Bad Men and Good: A Roundup of Western
Writers of America.* New York: Dodd, Mead, 1953. Humorously
antiacademic, superficial.
"What Editors Want in Western Covers," *Roundup,* December 1955,
pp. 3–5. Urges authenticity and "a fresh slant in packaging."
"Ernest Haycox: An Appreciation," *Call Number,* 25 (Fall 1963—
Spring, 1964), 2–3. Laudatory, brief.

4.   Publications with Short as Editor (Chronological)
Cattle, Guns & Men. New York: Bantam, 1955. No introduction.
Frontier: 150 Years of the West. New York: Bantam, 1955. No
introduction.
Colt's Law. New York: Bantam, 1957. No introduction.
Rawhide & Bob-Wire. New York: Bantam, 1958. No introduction.

5.   Unpublished Materials and Collections

The Fred D. Glidden Papers are in the Special Collections section of the Library of the University of Oregon, at Eugene, Oregon. They are in six parts: correspondence, clippings, manuscripts, magazine and newspaper pieces, books, and teleplays. The correspondence includes about three thousand letters. Most of them are between Glidden and his New York literary agent Marguerite E. Harper (dated 1934-66). Some are between Glidden and his Hollywood agent H. N. Swanson (and his aides, dated 1941-66). Others are between Glidden and various publishers (Ajax Music Company, 1952-53; Bantam Books, 1956-65; Dell, 1953-65; Houghton Mifflin, 1946-47; Macmillan, 1941-46; and *Saturday Evening Post*, 1940-50). Included are letters from fans, relating to Jonathan H. Glidden, to and from staff of the "Zane Grey Theater," and from others; and royalty statements, contracts, copyright assignments, copyright reports, and legal papers. The clippings are scattered reviews and notices. The manuscripts are original and carbon copies of twenty-seven novels (one unpublished, some with plot synopses and fragmentary working notes), twenty-five short stories (some unpublished), seven teleplays (some unsold), two screenplays (one unsold), one musical comedy (unsold), one article (unpublished), and about fifteen untitled fiction manuscripts of various lengths. The magazine and newspaper pieces are the first published appearances of about seventy items. The books, almost fifty in number, are mostly paperback editions, but also include some foreign translations and comic-book adaptations. The teleplays are five in number, were produced by the "Zane Grey Theater," and are published.

SECONDARY SOURCES

1.   Bibliographies

"Inventory of the Papers of Fred D. Glidden (Luke Short), University of Oregon Library," 1966, 1967, 1969. Invaluable. Includes what amounts to an almost complete bibliography.

WHITLEDGE, FRED C. "Luke Short," *Hitching Rail*, 1 (February 1973), 1-7. The best bibliography available; incomplete.

2.   Books

BOORSTIN, DANIEL J. *The Americans: The Democratic Experience.* New York: Random House, 1973; Vintage, 1974. Discusses late-nineteenth-century cattlemen as go-getters, in a class with oil barons, lawyers, gamblers, and professional criminals.

BROWN, DEE. *The Gentle Tamers: Women of the Old Wild West.* Lincoln: University of Nebraska Press, 1958. Surveys the important functions and influence women had in the Old West.

CAWELTI, JOHN G. *Adventures, Mystery, and Romance: Formula Stories as Art and Popular Culture.* Chicago and London: University of Chicago Press, 1976. Analyzes and criticizes popular-story formulas behind detective, spy, romance, and Western fiction, movies, and television series.

DURHAM, PHILIP, and JONES, EVERETT L. *The Negro Cowboys.* New York: Dodd, Mead, 1965. Discusses types of black cowboys and their contribution from Texas to Montana; deplores their having "been fenced out" of most Western fiction.

FOLSOM, JAMES K. *The American Western Novel.* New Haven: College & University Press, 1966. Treats selected Western novels as myths or fables, rather than realistic accounts; praises Short.

GRUBER, FRANK. *The Pulp Jungle.* Los Angeles: Sherbourne, 1967. Tells how one pulp writer made it to the big time; praises Short.

HARTE, BARBARA, and RILEY, CAROLYN, eds. "Glidden, Frederick D(illey)," pp. 209-10, in *Contemporary Authors,* vols. 21-22. Detroit: Gale Research, 1969. Contains basic biographical and bibliographical information.

JONES, DARYL. *The Dime Novel Western.* Bowling Green, Ohio: Popular Press, 1978. Shows the prepulp market out of which the pulps and then Short emerged.

LAMAR, HOWARD R., ed. *The Reader's Encyclopedia of the American West.* New York: Crowell, 1977. Useful in a thousand ways.

NYE, RUSSEL. *The Unembarrassed Muse: The Popular Arts in America.* New York: Dial, 1970. Links cowboy literature with detective and science fiction; discusses the development of Western literature chronologically.

OSGOOD, ERNEST STAPLES. *The Day of the Cattleman.* Minneapolis: University of Minnesota Press, 1929; rpt. Chicago and London: University of Chicago Press, n.d. Details the half-century history of range cattlemen, both wealthy herd owners and lonesome cowpunchers; discusses agricultural problems, trail driving, round-ups, rustlers, marketing, fencing, Indian difficulties, land ownership, cattlemen's associations, and railroads.

REYNOLDS, QUENTIN. *The Fiction Factory: or, From Pulp Row to Quality Street: The Story of 100 Years of Publishing at Street & Smith.* New York: Random House, 1955. Discusses Street & Smith's pulp magazines, including the ones publishing Westerns.

SEIDMAN, LAURENCE IVAN. *Once in the Saddle: The Cowboy's Frontier 1866-1896.* New York: Knopf, 1973; rpt. New York and Scarborough, Ontario: New American Library, 1973. Recreates the Old West days from diaries, autobiographical and descriptive accounts, photographs, and songs.

SMITH, HENRY NASH. *Virgin Land: The American West as Symbol and Myth.* Cambridge: Harvard University Press, 1950; rpt. New York:

Vintage, 1957. Studies how the nineteenth-century American West helped shape American social life and character; discusses the frontier, Manifest Destiny, Western heroes, and the West as garden.

SONNICHSEN, C. L. *From Hopalong to Hud: Thoughts on Western Fiction.* College Station, Texas, and London: Texas A & M University Press, 1978. Contains separate essays; relates to Short for its discussion of violence and sex in modern Westerns and for its treatment of the thin line between commercial and serious Western fiction.

3. Articles

DEVOTO, BERNARD. "Phaëthon on Gunsmoke Trail," *Harper's,* December 1954, pp. 10-11, 14, 16. Ridicules horse-opera clichés.

ETULAIN, RICHARD W. "The Historical Development of the Western," *Journal of Popular Culture,* 7 (Winter 1973), 717-26. Categorizes and elucidates, moves chronologically, but is too brief.

FRAZEE, STEVE. "Meet Fred Glidden," *Roundup,* October 1955, pp. 3-4. Offers early biographical data.

GARFIELD, BRIAN. "The Fiddlefoot from Kewanee," *Roundup,* November 1975, pp. 6-7, 11. Offers gentle eulogy by a knowledgeable friend.

GURIAN, JAY. "The Unwritten West," *American West,* 2 (Winter 1965), 59-63. Rebukes the media for glamorizing and fantasizing the West, thus converting it from "great" to merely "wild."

"Keeping Posted," *Saturday Evening Post,* March 15, 1941, p. 4. Gives biographical and autobiographical material regarding Short, with photographs, as lead material to the first serial installment of his *Blood on the Moon* (novel title: *Gunman's Chance*).

"Luke Short Again Whacking the Keys," *Roundup,* August 1971, pp. 8, 16. Discusses Short's research into real-life Colorado background of *The Outrider* (and touches on Aspen background of *Silver Rock*).

"Luke Short Dead: Wrote Westerns," *New York Times,* August 19, 1975, p. 36. Presents laudatory obituary notice.

"Luke Short Dies at 67: Was Long a Member of WWA," *Roundup,* October 1975, p. 10. Offers tender tribute.

OLSEN, T. V. "Luke Short, Writer's Writer," *Roundup,* March 1973, pp. 10-11, 13. Praises Short for being a personal influence; contrasts Short and Ernest Haycox; and singles out *And the Wind Blows Free, Ambush,* and *Ride the Man Down* for their special stylistic excellences.

THOMAS, PHILLIP D. "The Paperback West of Luke Short," *Journal of Popular Culture,* 7 (Winter 1973), 701-708. Briefly discusses Short's depiction of frontier communities and character stereotypes; offers evidence from only eight novels.

WALKER, DON D. "Notes toward a Literary Criticism of the Western,"
Journal of Popular Culture, 7 (Winter 1973), 728–41. Challenges
the critics to analyze Westerns for their skillful plotting, use of
chance as a theme, and allegorical elements.

Index